Junior Youth Activities for the Lent and Easter Seasons

An Interactive Guide to Discovering Spirituality

Steve Mason

Sandy Rigsby

Resource Publications, Inc.
San Jose, California

Reprint Department
Resource Publications, Inc.
160 E. Virginia Street #290
San Jose, CA 95112-5876
(408) 286-8505 voice
(408) 287-8748 fax

Library of Congress Cataloging-in-Publication Data
Mason, Steve, 1960 May 15–
    Junior youth activities for the Lent and Easter seasons : an interactive guide to discovering spirituality / Steve Mason, Sandy Rigsby.
        p.   cm. — (Awakening the Word series)
    Includes indexes.
    ISBN 0-89390-510-0
    1. Church group work with youth. 2. Catechetics—Catholic Church. 3. Lent—Study and teaching (Middle school)
4. Eastertide—Study and teaching (Middle school) 5. Bible. N.T. Gospels—Study and teaching (Middle school)
I. Rigsby, Sandy, 1960– II. Title. III. Series.

BX2347.8.Y7 M37 2001
268'.432—dc21

                                                                                                    2001048340

Printed in the United States of America.
01 02 03 04 05 | 5 4 3 2 1

Editorial director: Nick Wagner
Production: Romina Saha
Copyeditor: Tricia Joerger
Cover design: Nelson Estarija

Contents

Appendixes

Preface

It was 12:20 in the afternoon; he was twenty minutes late for the luncheon. "Oh no, this is a great first impression to make," he thought rolling into the parking lot. She was pacing the floor in the large mall, waiting. "He did say 12:00, didn't he? Was this the place we were to meet or did I somehow misunderstand? What a great way to start this co-catechist experience," she thought. After a few more minutes and an embarrassing question to a passing stranger, he finally made an appearance.

With nervous formalities, introductions, and an apology or two, we finally met for the first time. We came together to discuss our thoughts and make plans for the coming year. Little did we know what type of journey awaited us. Like catechists in many parishes, we came together to simply share our faith with the younger generation. We were not authors, theologians, educators, or child experts. We were each parents with children enrolled in the parish program, a religious formation program that depended on everyday people to come forward and share their faith.

As we discussed our thoughts about teaching over lunch, it became apparent we held in common some rather simple goals. First, we wanted to make the sessions fun. We wanted the youth to enjoy coming to religious education instead of it being something they dreaded each week. Second, we wanted the sessions to be relevant to the youth. We felt that our material needed to be presented in a way that made sense to young adolescents. We also wanted the youth to be able to apply the Scriptures to situations in their real world, common events that happen at school or home. Finally, we felt it was important to instill a sense of community with the group. In our parish the youth attended a number of different local schools. We wanted them to get to know one another and become friends with each other. We wanted our meeting room to become a place where they could experience faith and enthusiasm among their peers. With these ideologies in common and the shaky start behind us, we were ready to take on the challenge of sharing our faith with sixth graders.

As the year progressed we discovered unique ways to bring fun and relevance to our lessons while managing to foster a sense of community with the youth. Between us we had several years experience as catechists, yet we were constantly challenged to live up to the goals we had set. By the end of the year we were amazed at what had unfolded. By using a different approach, the youth developed an enthusiasm for catechesis and retained material from the very earliest sessions. Equally amazing and rewarding were the comments and support that came from parents. They spoke of how their children had a change of attitude toward religious education. In many cases the youth told their parents how they looked forward to the activities each week.

After nearly two years of teaching together, we realized we were onto something. A unique way to approach religious education was evolving: an approach that could be used in various forms of adolescent youth ministry as well. However, just as we were finding our stride, changes were in the air; changes that would take this journey down a different path. In our second year of team teaching, a job transfer put an end to our time as co-catechists.

As we parted ways, the idea of putting our techniques, activities, and philosophies into print picked up momentum. Thanks to the support and encouraging words of many people, we decided to share these activities with others in this book.

The goals for this book are quite similar to those we set for teaching. We want to create an easy-to-use resource for catechists, junior youth leaders, and catechumenate leaders; a resource to help bring fun, relevance, and a sense of community to the youth they serve.

We have developed and tested activities that youth in fifth through eighth grade find engaging. Each session is centered on an activity. These activities are based upon the Sunday Gospels (except for Ascension and Pentecost which are based upon the first reading from Acts) and are designed to let the youth enter into an experience that parallels an experience or theme from the reading. For most passages the activity attempts to create an experience from an individual's perspective. This may be a disciple, Jesus, or perhaps someone Jesus healed. Actions and experiences in the activity symbolically parallel the featured person's perspective from the reading.

The youth find this fun for a couple of reasons. First, they get to do something. How often is youth ministry or catechesis scheduled after school or in the evenings? By this time, most youth have spent all day in school and much of their time between school and religious education doing homework. Another hour or so of sitting still and listening is not something they get excited about. God has blessed them with abundant energy and they want to use it. These activities often take place outside the meeting room and may feature running or other forms of exercise. Leaving the meeting room is to a youth what leaving the workplace is to an adult. Second, the activities often encourage them to work together to meet some type of challenge. They are recognized and affirmed for their efforts. Teamwork, challenges, exercise, recognition, and affirmation, these are the things youth enjoy.

We have also strived to make this material relevant, memorable, and meaningful for the youth. After the activity, the group moves to a quiet place for reflection and discussion. This second half of the session begins with the Scripture passage read aloud to the youth. What follows is a group discussion moderated by the leader. The Scripture is explored in the context of their recent experiences in the activity. The youth are challenged to bring out the similarities between the activity and the reading. In this way, Scripture comes alive to them; it is perceived as something to be experienced. They are allowed to enter into the perspective of someone featured in the reading and let it speak to them on the level of experience.

Discussion questions are designed to allow the youth to discover and pull out spiritual truths in their own words. While the reflection is guided by the leader, the emphasis is always on the youth making the connections and verbalizing them. In this way, instead of being told what to believe, the youth form their own insights based on the Scripture. When they discover the truth themselves, it becomes much more meaningful to them. Questions are also designed to let the youth bridge these truths with experiences from their everyday lives. They are challenged to come up with practical ways to live consistently with the truths they have identified. In this way, spirituality and Scripture are experienced as relevant to them; it speaks to situations they face daily.

Our final goal is to foster a sense of community with the youth. Playing together, sharing experiences together, having fun together, and exploring the Scriptures together all help create a sense of unity among the youth. Also, by placing youth on different teams and in different small groups each week, the youth meet and become familiar with all youth in the group. We have also found that good preparation beforehand allows the catechist to greet the youth as they gather. Welcoming them and being present to them at this time creates a sense of community that sets the tone for the entire period.

We designed these sessions with a simple two-part format: an activity followed by a reflection period. Each part emphasizes important fundamentals of spiritual growth. The activity emphasizes spirituality as an experience. The Gospels are filled with experiences of significant meaning. Our relationship with God is an experience of love. While academics are important to faith, it is also important to let the youth discover faith and spirituality as an experience. Following the activity with a reflection period lets the youth develop the habit of reflecting on the events of their own lives. In asking meaningful questions, the youth discover the connections and relevance between Scriptures and their own experiences. It empowers them to take ownership of these truths as something they have found and experienced.

We sincerely hope you find this resource helpful in your ministry. Your willingness to share your faith is a wonderful witness of your own spiritual journey. Know that we feel a certain kinship with you as our spiritual paths cross in the sessions of this book. May the Spirit guide you in your work and lead you to God's presence in all the people you meet.

Acknowledgments

We have encountered many wonderful people along our journey, people whose encouragement, support, creativity, and help have made this book possible. The following people have contributed in a significant way to this work:

Nick Wagner believed in us and gave us the opportunity to share our thoughts.

Wanda Scheuermann's creativity and direction helped us formulate this vision.

Our readers reviewed the work and made it better with their insightful comments.
Father Jeffrey Donner
Janice Lovecchio
Elaine McCarron, SCN
Patrica Mueller
Bob Ostenfeld
Sister Janet Schaeffler, OP
Sister Maureen Shaughnessy, SC

Our families supported us throughout all the hours of typing and long-distance phone calls. We sincerely appreciate your patience.
Joe, Carla, Michelle, and Matt Rigsby
Jane, Philip, Matthew, and Kathleen Mason

Many youth in Tennessee and Michigan taught us much of what it means to minister in religious formation. For these bright and fun young people we give thanks.

Introduction

How to Use This Book

For whom this book is written

This book is designed as a resource for catechists and ministers working with youth between ten and fourteen years of age (fifth through eighth grades.) The material is particularly well suited for religious education classes, retreats, days of recollection, junior youth ministry meetings, and children's catechumenate during the extended catechetical sessions.

The liturgical seasons

Each session focuses upon the Gospel reading for a particular Sunday of Lent or Easter (except those for Ascension and Pentecost which use the first reading from Acts.) Parishes that base their religious education, RCIA, and youth ministry activities on the Sunday lectionary readings will find sessions for the entire Lent and Easter seasons.

In parishes using non-lectionary based curriculum, the cross-reference sections make it easy to use these sessions to supplement a theme or explore a Scripture passage.

This book focuses only on the Lent and Easter seasons; other books in this series will focus on the rest of the liturgical calendar. Sessions are provided for Sundays in each of the three years of the liturgical cycle. In some cases one session may be used for the same Sunday in all three liturgical years. A liturgical calendar has been included to help easily identify which session to use on any given date during the Lent and Easter seasons.

How the sessions are structured

The sessions are divided into two parts: an activity followed by a group discussion period. (Palm Sunday is the exception.) The activities may take place outside, in a gymnasium, throughout the parish facility, or in a meeting room. By contrast, the discussion period is held in a separate area preferably away from the activity site. Day chapels, side chapels, churches, and quiet areas outside are ideal for this reflection and discussion time.

The written sessions have been formatted to anticipate the sequence a catechist or youth leader may follow to plan a session. Each session is titled for a particular Sunday and liturgical year. A word or two stating the general theme along with the lectionary readings for the Sunday are provided next. These headings make it easy to quickly identify the session, its theme, and the Scripture passages on which it is based. Choosing the correct session should be simple.

The next step in preparing a session is to become familiar with the material. The Theme section begins by instructing the leader to read the appropriate Scripture passage. Two or three paragraphs are then provided to explore the themes and establish a context for the session. In the second half of this section, the Scripture passage is explored through questions designed for the youth. The focus here shifts toward the youth's perspective. These questions highlight important areas of discovery for the youth and allow the leader to begin reflecting on how to best facilitate this discovery.

The themes and activities in this book rely on a metaphorical approach to Scriptures. Certainly other interpretations are accurate, but the point here is to make simple and direct connections between the youth and Scriptures. Typically two or three main themes are featured to keep it practical and age appropriate.

With the theme well established, the next step in the process is to move from the abstract to the concrete. Two short sections of each session are dedicated specifically to this transition.

The Activity Summary section begins this process by introducing the activity to the leader. Here the goals of the activity are expressed and a brief description of the activity is provided. The transition is made more concrete in the section entitled Bridging the Activity and Reading. This section is composed of three or four points showing how a bridge will be formed between the reading and activity. After reading these three sections, the leader should be well acquainted with the Scripture passage, have a good idea what the activity is about, and understand how the activity relates to the Scripture.

The next step is to begin preparing for the activity. The Preparation section offers detailed steps of everything the leader must do to prepare for the activity. Instructions are also provided on how to introduce the activity to the youth and guide them through it. A Supply List section is included listing all the supplies needed for the activity.

At this point, the leader has everything in place for the activity and is ready to focus on the group discussion. This second part of the session provides the youth an opportunity to reflect on their experiences and discover the truths contained within the Scripture passage.

The Reflection section instructs the leader to begin by reading aloud the featured Scripture passage. Once everyone has listened to the reading, the leader guides the group in discussion. The questions provided in the Questions for Discussion section are specifically designed to let the youth verbalize their insights and uncover meaning in the Scriptures. Questions typically fall into one of three categories: questions to explore the Scripture passage; questions to explore the activity; and questions to explore the relevance of these truths in life. Often the questions are grouped in a way that builds one upon another in order to help explore a particular theme. Emphasis is always upon the youth discovering and verbalizing. The leader's role here is to facilitate the youth's discovery of truth.

The final section of each session is designed for children's catechumenate leaders. The Catechumenate Connection section can be used in the extended catechetical sessions to explore themes, sacraments, and traditions of the Catholic Church. The topics and questions provided here are intended to supplement the questions found in the Questions for Discussion section. One goal of this section is to introduce the youth to the teachings of the church. The *Catechism of the Catholic Church* is referenced often and should be readily available to accompany this section.

How to use this material in your ministry

This book is designed for use in four different youth ministries: religious education, days of recollection or retreats, junior youth ministry programs, and children's catechumenate programs. This section discusses how to efficiently use this book as a resource in these ministries.

Many parishes follow the liturgical cycle as the basis for their various ministries. Such parishes use the Sunday readings and its themes as the focus for these ministries. This book is easily adaptable to this format. The sessions are clearly marked in the heading to correspond to each of the Sundays of Lent and Easter. The Liturgical Calendar in the appendix matches each date of the Sundays in Lent and Easter with the corresponding session to be used through the year 2030. Since the sessions take about an hour and fifteen minutes to complete, catechists and ministers may simply use these as their entire session during these seasons. If another liturgical-based curriculum is used in the program, these sessions may be used to supplement or add variety.

Parishes using curriculum not based on the Sunday liturgical readings may also wish to supplement their programs with these sessions. These curriculums often explore themes or Scriptures central to the faith, themes that may be found throughout this book. Days of recollection and retreat experiences may also be dedicated to exploring certain themes and Scriptures. In both of these cases, the three cross-reference sections in the appendixes will be helpful.

Often a catechist or minister may need an activity or discussion questions to help explore a particular Scripture passage. The Index of Scripture Passages was designed with this in mind. Each Scripture passage is listed in order along with the corresponding Sunday title, activity, and page number. This tool is particularly helpful in planning activities around a specific Scripture passage.

The Cross-Reference by Theme alphabetically lists each theme explored in this book. For every theme one or more sessions are available to choose from. The corresponding activity, Sunday title, and page number are provided to make finding the specific session easy. A catechist or minister looking for an idea or an activity to fit a theme needs to simply look here for several ideas. The Index of Sessions lists all the Sundays of Lent and Easter in chronological order. Again the corresponding activity and themes are listed.

This book has also been designed for use in extended catechetical sessions of the children's catechumenate process. The lectionary-based format of this book makes it easily adaptable for this ministry. Often, however, parishes have few youth in this age group going through the process at any given time. These limited numbers may require the catechist to creatively change the activities to accommodate the small group. At other times it may be impossible to do the activity. In these cases, the Reflection section of the session along with the Questions for Discussion and the Catechumenate Connection sections can still be used. Some discussion questions, however, should be omitted if the activity is not used.

The Catechumenate Connection Cross-Reference in the appendix lists the Sundays in chronological order along with the corresponding topic, Catholic tradition, and sacraments to be discussed in each week's Catechumenate Connection section. These sections are provided at the end of each session specifically for use in RCIA. Since these youth are exploring the Catholic faith, the *Catechism of the Catholic Church* is referenced extensively as a resource. The various sections of this document used for discussion are listed for each week in the Catechumenate Connection Cross-Reference and Cross-Reference by Section of the CCC. These cross-references are not only helpful in planning RCIA, but can be used as idea resources for exploring any of the topics, sacraments, and traditions of Catholicism.

These cross-references can quickly provide ideas on many themes. If more information is needed about a particular session or activity, the Activity Summary section in each session can be used for a quick synopsis.

Tips for Getting the Most Out of These Sessions

Sometimes a little bit of knowledge can go a long way. In developing and using these sessions we discovered a few pearls that significantly enhance the quality of these experiences. What follows are a few tips to enrich the activities, build community with the group, and make the sessions more meaningful.

Preparation is the key. There simply is no substitute for good preparation. Being well prepared with all the details arranged before the group gathers brings a myriad of benefits. There is a peace and calm that comes with knowing everything is ready. This peace is sensed by the youth and allows the leader to be more present as they gather. It also sets the tone for the session and communicates something about the importance and value of what is to be experienced.

The leader's spiritual preparation is essential. In addition to attending to the physical arrangements, preparation also means spending time with the Scripture passage. Always read the full passage and allow the word to soak into your soul. Take time to reflect on the questions in the theme section. When the Scriptures move you and speak to your life, you are ready to facilitate the youth's discovery.

Gathering time is an opportunity to build community. Make the gathering experience fun and welcoming for the youth. Greet each youth as they enter, be present to them, ask about their day, and invite them to enter the conversation. One way to create fun is to ask faith trivia questions, tossing candy to anyone answering correctly. Be spontaneous and join in the fun. Laugh easily, be genuine and the youth will respond in the same way. Be mindful of the journey of discovery they are about to experience and let its excitement and energy set the tone in these early moments.

Open and close with prayer. Experiencing group prayer brings spirituality and community together. Reflect upon the theme of the session and let the Spirit work through you in prayer. These prayers can be simple and short or quite involved experiences if you wish. There is value in exposing the youth to various forms of prayer and allowing them to lead the prayer if they are comfortable doing so. If you lead a prayer, pray with passion and meaning. Never underestimate the powerful influence you have when youth witness you in prayer.

Challenge the youth to listen to the readings at Mass. If this material is used weekly, explain that the activity in each week's session will have something to do with the Gospel from Sunday Mass. Invite them to participate in the celebration of the word by paying careful attention to the readings and the homily. Consider tossing candy during the gathering to anyone able to explain what happened in the readings. Another idea is to make listening to the Sunday readings a standing expectation throughout the year.

Explain the format of the session to the youth. Let them know the session has two parts, an activity and reflection. Explain how the activity is designed to be fun yet filled with meaning from the Scriptures. This differs from the reflection period, which is a quieter time when the group discusses the activity and the Scripture passage. Make it clear they are expected to transition from the louder energy of the activity to a quieter disposition during the reflection period.

Choose the activity site carefully. Look for a site that is particularly well suited for the activity. If an outside site is chosen, be sure to have a contingency plan for inclement weather. Be considerate of other groups or ministries that may be meeting in your facility at the time of your activity. Excessive noise can be disruptive. In selecting an indoor site, be mindful of the space requirement and be sensitive to the environmental impact your group could have on the space. Pastors tend to be more supportive when their maintenance budgets are left intact.

Adapt the activities to fit your facility, resources, and space. At times the activity may call for resources or space that is unavailable in your facility. Creativity and a good understanding of the activity goals will allow you to change parts of the activity while retaining the integrity of the intended experience. The activities have been designed to use relatively inexpensive items frequently found at home or in the facility's supply closet. Often, suitable substitutes are readily available.

Tailor the sessions to fit the needs of your youth. These sessions are designed to anticipate the needs of catechists and youth, however, there are many situations that are impossible to predict. In these cases, tailor the content, activities, reflection, and awards in ways that meet your youth's needs. For example, if a particular activity seems too risky, follow your judgment and change it. If one or more youth in your group has diabetes or dental needs, reconsider awarding candy. Likewise, if rewarding candy seems unnecessary to create motivation, consider sincere words of recognition and affirmation as a substitute. If you find candy adds significant motivation for your youth, consider using it in more sessions. If your youth discuss the readings openly, feel free to use only a few of the questions or create your own.

Reserve a quiet place for the reflection period away from the activity site. Day chapels, side chapels, churches, and quiet areas outside are ideal for the reflection period. Letting the youth physically move to a quieter environment helps them make the transition. Choose a site that will not be interrupted by others and lends itself to quiet discussion.

Always begin the reflection period by reading the Scripture passage aloud. These sessions are based upon the Sunday Gospel or first reading. The reflection period is designed to let the youth explore the word. Consider having an adult leader or someone with good public reading skills read the passage. Coach the lector to speak slowly and clearly in such a way that all who are gathered can easily hear. Using a lectionary and beginning with the familiar, "A reading from the holy Gospel according to …" and ending with, "The Gospel of the Lord" followed by the response, is a wonderful way to make this reflection period an extension of the liturgical celebration of the word. Be sure to use an age-appropriate Scripture source to ensure the youth can understand the text.

Let the youth discover the relevance and truth in Scripture. These sessions have been created in the spirit of discovery. The leader's role is to facilitate this discovery. Allow the youth to verbalize how the activity related to the Scripture. The section Bridging the Activity and Reading lists the key symbolisms, but the intent is to have the youth make these connections. In the same way, let the youth uncover the truths in Scriptures. Let them articulate their insights of how these truths have meaning in their lives. When the youth make the discovery and express it, they begin to take ownership. Open-ended questions, patience, and affirmation help facilitate this discovery.

Be prepared to use closed-ended questions to jump-start the discussion. Reflecting on activities, feelings, and Scriptures is an acquired skill, one the youth must develop. Expect them to be somewhat reticent as they begin, especially the first couple of times this material is used. If this happens, consider re-phrasing some questions to help jump-start the discussion. Closed-ended questions, those they answer with a *yes* or *no,* may be less threatening for a youth to answer in front of others. Follow these closed-ended questions by asking them to explain their answer. Questions beginning with the word *why* work nicely. For example, suppose the youth cannot think of an answer for the question: *What are some ways to strengthen yourself against temptation?* Consider rewording the question to: *Do you think prayer can help strengthen you against temptation? Why?* Finally, ask the original question again: *What else do you think strengthens you against temptation?* Be sure to be affirming, let them know they answered well, and get excited when they make the connections. If the group is having trouble making a final discovery or connection in a series of questions, summarize the things they have expressed to that point. Allow them to see the logical sequence of their discoveries.

Be flexible and recognize the Spirit at work. It will quickly become apparent using this experience and discovery model that unexpected things can happen. Maybe a surprise alternative emerges in an activity, an unanticipated connection or revelation is discovered in the discussion, or perhaps a youth finds special meaning in something that was unintended. The best advice at these times is to be flexible and look for the Spirit at work. The Spirit's agenda exists independently of ours. More discovery and meaning may be found by taking a side path on the discussion. The important thing here is to develop a discerning eye for the Spirit's presence.

While these tips are designed to enhance these sessions, the real key to creating meaningful experiences is recognizing God's presence in our lives. Be mindful that these sessions have been written in the spirit of discovery, a spirit that senses the fun and significance in finding the connection between scriptural truths and ordinary experiences. Perhaps the best and final tip, however, is to remain prayerful as you prepare for and share your journey.

Part 1: Lent

1st Sunday of Lent (ABC)

Temptation   ✝   *Perseverance*

Readings

A	B	C
Genesis 2:7–9; 3:1–7	Genesis 9:8–15	Deuteronomy 26:4–10
Psalm 51:3–4, 5–6, 12–13, 17	Psalm 25:4–5, 6–7, 8–9	Psalm 91:1–2, 10–11, 12–13, 14–15
Romans 5:12–19	1 Peter 3:18–22	Romans 10:8–13
Matthew 4:1–11	Mark 1:12–15	Luke 4:1–13

Theme

Read Matthew 4:1–11, Mark 1:12–15, or Luke 4:1–13. The Lenten season opens with the story of Jesus entering the desert for forty days of fasting and temptation. What an appropriate image to usher us into the season of preparation for new life. As Jesus grew closer to God in the desert in order to be of better service to the world, so, too, we follow his example in Lent by assuming a penitential spirit through fasting and prayer. Catechumens are invited to enter their name into the Book of the Elect on this First Sunday of Lent in preparation for their baptism at Easter. The faithful recall their own baptism as a means of strengthening themselves against temptations.

Each year of the liturgical cycle features a different Gospel account of this temptation narrative on the First Sunday of Lent. In Years A and C, Matthew and Luke provide rich detail of the temptations, while in year B, Mark gives only a brief summary of the event. Regardless of the liturgical year, the Gospel theme for this Sunday is learning how to understand what tempts us and to persevere in the presence of temptation.

Looking at the text closely, it is clear Jesus relied on God's word recorded in Scripture to strengthen him against temptation. Allow the youth to discover this truth and invite them to explore ways they, too, can strengthen themselves against today's temptations.

Jesus faced several types of temptation in the desert: misusing power, worshiping false gods, and putting God to the test. What temptations can the youth describe in their lives? How do they handle such temptations? How do they feel about struggling with temptation? How does the community help them resist temptation? When do they feel most vulnerable to temptation?

Each of the Gospel accounts describes Jesus as being filled with the Holy Spirit and being led by the Spirit into the desert to face temptation. Do we not pray in the Lord's Prayer to be led not into temptation? What is this all about? Why would the Holy Spirit lead

Jesus into this situation? How do the youth see Christians being called to face temptation? How do the youth see the Holy Spirit strengthening them to face worldly values?

Activity Summary

The activity is designed to allow the youth an opportunity to explore the experience of temptation. Their challenge will be to resist the desire to drink water throughout the activity. Several layers of temptations are designed to heighten their thirst and break their resolve. Lead the activity so that no youth feels weak or guilty giving into the temptation. The intent is not to create guilt but to provide them with an appreciation for Jesus' temptation and to become more aware of temptations in their everyday lives.

Bridging the Activity and Reading

- ☐ The temptation to drink symbolizes Jesus' temptations in the desert.
- ☐ Creating thirst by exercising and eating salty foods parallels Jesus' fast in the desert.
- ☐ The leader's temptations in the activity represent the devil's temptations in the Gospel.
- ☐ The youth resisting the temptation to drink represents Jesus resisting the devil's temptations.

Preparation

Preparation is simple. Fill a pitcher with water and gather a clear drinking glass, paper plate, and napkin for each youth. Next, bring a variety of salty snack foods for each youth to eat heartily. Pretzels, saltine crackers, popcorn, and potato chips work very well—the saltier the better. If they do not have much salt, add some yourself. Also, bring hot salsa for those wanting to live on the edge. With these items gathered, you are now ready to begin.

Announce to the group they will be undergoing a test of resolve. Everyone will be tempted to drink water. Those strong enough to successfully resist the temptation will be recognized. Announce that there are only two rules: First, everyone must do exactly as the leader says, no matter what it may be. The only exception to this would be if the leader should tell them to take a drink of anything. In this case, and only in this case, they must disobey. Second, and this is the real test, no one is allowed to take a single drink of anything until the test is over. The only way to know if the test is over is by listening for the words, *The devil is now tired of all this tempting and will await another opportunity later.* Write this phrase on the chalkboard. Explain again that until the leader says these words, the test continues and no drinking is allowed.

Once everyone understands the object and rules, begin by announcing, *The test is now underway.* Place the pitcher of water and glasses on a table in front of the group. Pouring a glass of water ask the youth, *Who would like a glass of water?* Walk around the room offering the glass to each of them. The idea is to genuinely try to get them to drink. Remember, this activity requires the leader to become the tempter. Assume the tempter attitude by explaining how the water is nice and cold. Tell the youth it is fresh spring water as pure as water gets. Ask them to take a drink. Suggest to them individually how they must be thirsty and really want a drink of water. Again, offer the glass to each youth.

This first temptation should be relatively easy to resist. Make a mental note, however, of anyone giving into the temptation. These youth should be allowed to continue; their example of drinking can be used to tempt others later.

Next, take the group outside, or, if possible, to a gymnasium or large indoor area. Explain to them how their speed and endurance are now going to be tested. Have the youth run several sprints together. An alternative activity may be a game of basketball, soccer, or tag. Whatever you decide, remember the idea is to get them winded and thirsty. Keep an eye on the time, since quite a bit still needs to be covered in this period. Ten to fifteen minutes should be sufficient.

Once completed, return to the room for the second round of temptations. Go through the room again offering the glass of water to all the thirsty youth. Tell them how running must have made them so terribly thirsty. Ask them to imagine just how great it would feel to have a nice tall glass of water. At this point take a drink yourself in front of them. Carry on about how good the water tastes and how you are now quite refreshed and ready to go.

This second temptation should be a bit more difficult to resist. Do not be surprised if one or two fail. Do not overreact or look shamefully upon these youth. Instead, encourage others to follow suit. After all, as tempter, your goal is to get all the youth to take a drink.

Next, tell them you have a little treat for everyone. Distribute plates, napkins, salty snacks, and the hot salsa. Explain that everyone must take and eat a full plate of the snacks. Offer a serving of hot salsa to anyone up to the challenge. While they are enjoying their snacks, take a glass of water and one of the youth outside the room. Offer this lone youth a drink. Explain how you know he or she is very thirsty and no others are watching. Continue to tempt the youth by making him or her hold the glass. After a sufficient time, have the youth return to the room and call for another to come out. Repeat this individual temptation for each youth.

This third temptation should be the most difficult to resist. Not only are both the exercising and salty snacks working to build their thirst, they also no longer have the group encouragement to help resist this private temptation. Expect to have a few fall for this one.

When all have been tempted individually, return to the room and begin telling them how the exercising and salty snacks must really be making them thirsty. Again, offer each youth a drink. Then, in your most authoritative voice, announce that the simulation is over (do not, however, say the magic words!) and everyone can now have as much water as they want. Pour a glass of water for each youth and tell them you must step out of the room for just a minute to check on something. They can help themselves to the water while you are out. Leave the room for a minute or two. Upon returning, ask if anyone took a drink of water.

This final temptation attempts to trick the youth and give them the opportunity to get away with something in the absence of authority. Of course, you will just have to believe them about the results while you were gone.

At this point the test is over. Announce clearly and loudly, *The devil is now tired of all this tempting and will await another opportunity later.* With this, give each of the youth a much-deserved drink of water. Bring forward those who have remained faithful to the end and have the group give a big round of applause. Congratulate each one by name for their faithfulness. It is now time to move to the reflection area.

Supply List

- ☐ pitcher of water
- ☐ clear drinking glasses, enough for each youth and leaders
- ☐ paper plates and napkins for each youth
- ☐ variety of salty snacks such as pretzels, saltine crackers, popcorn, and potato chips
- ☐ hot salsa
- ☐ soccer ball or basketball (optional)

Reflection

Read aloud Matthew 4:1–11, Mark 1:12–15, or Luke 4:1–13.

Questions for Discussion

- ☐ What did the activity have to do with the Gospel?
- ☐ How did you overcome the temptation in the activity?
- ☐ In the Gospel, how was Jesus able to resist the temptations?
- ☐ What are some ways you can strengthen yourself against temptation?
- ☐ What kinds of temptation did Jesus face in the desert?
- ☐ Describe some of the temptation people your age face today.
- ☐ How do people your age handle these temptations?
- ☐ How do you feel about struggling with temptation?
- ☐ In the activity, when was it most difficult to resist temptation?
- ☐ When do you feel most vulnerable to temptation in your life?
- ☐ What was it like in the activity to be tempted alone outside the room?
- ☐ What role do other people have in tempting you and helping you resist temptation?
- ☐ During the last temptation, how did it feel to be tricked into believing the game was over?
- ☐ How did the devil try to trick Jesus in the desert?
- ☐ Why do you suppose the Holy Spirit led Jesus into the desert to be tempted?
- ☐ How does the Holy Spirit strengthen you to face worldly values?
- ☐ What have you discovered from this Gospel and how can you apply it in your life?
- ☐ In the next few days when you face temptation, what have you discovered today to help you resist it?

Catechumenate Connection

This First Sunday of Lent, catechumens are given the opportunity to record their name in the Book of the Elect announcing their intention to join the church at the Easter Vigil. The church consists of a community of believers. Explore the importance of community with the

- stick pretzels
- doritos : chips
- hot salsa
- popcorn
- sweet candy -

-

elect and catechumens. How does the faith community help us in our struggle against temptation? How does seeing others' faith help the youth with their faith? How would they feel if they were the only one who came to Mass on a given Sunday?

The word "fortitude" is described in the *Catechism of the Catholic Church* (§1808). Invite the youth to look up and discuss the virtue. What are ways to increase our fortitude?

Discuss how communal prayer strengthens people to face temptation. Explore how Catholics find God's presence four ways in the celebration of the Eucharist: God is present in the word, in the bread and wine, in the priest, and in the people gathered. Each of these experiences of God's presence helps build our faith and strengthens our fortitude. Invite the youth to imagine how this might work.

Talk about how Lent is a wonderful opportunity to strengthen our faith. How does fasting and prayer during Lent prepare them for initiation into the church? What are ways they can grow closer to God this Lent? What habits and activities can prevent us from taking time to listen to God? How can they become more prayerful? What are some ways to pray?

2nd Sunday of Lent (ABC)

Conversion	✝	*Trust*

Readings

A	B	C
Genesis 12:1–4a	Genesis 22:1–2, 9a, 10–13, 15–18	Genesis 15:5–12, 17–18
Psalm 33:4–5, 18–19, 20, 22	Psalm 116:10, 15, 16–17, 18–19	Psalm 27:1, 7–8, 8–9, 13–14
2 Timothy 1:8b–10	Romans 8:31b–34	Philippians 3:17–4:1 or 3:20–4:1
Matthew 17:1–9	Mark 9:2–10	Luke 9:28b–36

Theme

Read Matthew 17:1–9, Mark 9:2–10, or Luke 9:28b–36. This second week of Lent we are called to a deeper conversion. Just as Jesus was completely transfigured before the disciples, we, too, are invited to a complete transformation. Our Lenten transformation leaves us radiant with God's love and empowers us to descend from our safe mountains to face our daily crosses with courage and faith.

Each year of the liturgical cycle features a different account of Jesus' transfiguration on the Second Sunday of Lent. While these accounts are very similar, the accompanying readings seem to underscore various parts of the conversion theme. In Year A, the story of Abram leaving his homeland and risking everything at God's command speaks of the risks and trust required in conversion. In Year B, Abraham's willingness to sacrifice his own son speaks of the sacrifice and trust conversion demands. In Year C, God's covenant and faithfulness are emphasized in the story of Abram.

All three Gospel accounts speak of Jesus taking Peter, John, and James up a mountain. Luke says they went there to pray. Where do the youth go when they need to sort things out? Why is it beneficial to have a safe place where they can retreat from their busy lives? What role do quiet and prayer play in their spiritual growth?

The Gospels state that Jesus became transfigured before them and he appeared dazzling white. How do the youth act and feel different when they experience love? What are ways they see people act that reveal a change of heart?

As Moses and Elijah appeared, Peter, missing the point, suggested they erect tents to accommodate the visitors. What are some ways we try to control God? Hearing the Lord's voice, they became frightened. What is scary about change and growth in the youth's eyes? What things do they feel must be let go of in order to grow? How much risk are they willing to take to grow closer to God?

The miraculous cloud commanded them to listen to Jesus. After hearing this they descended the mountain. Where do the youth hear God speaking and how does this help their conversion? How do the youth feel about leaving their safe places and entering the world living God's word?

Activity Summary

The activity this second week of Lent is designed to allow youth to explore some of the dynamics of conversion. They can discover how growth requires leaving behind the safe and moving into risky areas of the unknown. They will get a chance to experience retreating to a safe place and returning again to vulnerability when the time is right. The objective is to invite the students to consider that change and conversion require being vulnerable and taking risks.

The activity is a game called Bermuda Triangle. The object of the game is to collect as many tokens as possible. The playing area consists of three safe zones or squares arranged around a basket of tokens that are guarded by a tagger. In the safe zone, the players are safe and cannot be tagged by the one designated as the tagger. In order to collect the tokens, the players must leave the safe zone, run to the middle, grab a token, and return to a safe zone without being tagged. If a player is tagged, that player must give one of his or her tokens to the tagger.

Bridging the Activity and Reading

- ☐ The safe zone symbolizes the mountain while the Bermuda Triangle represents returning to the risky world.
- ☐ Leaving the safe zone to get a token resembles Jesus leaving Moses and Elijah and the safety of the mountain.
- ☐ Leaving the safe zone, experiencing the risk of the Bermuda Triangle, and returning to the safe zone is an experience that changes each player in some way. In the Gospel, Jesus left the safety of his home, went into the world preaching a radical type of love that challenged the local religious leaders, then retreated to the safety of the mountain to pray. In doing this he, too, was transfigured.

Preparation

Begin by preparing the playing area. Choose a large area such as a gymnasium, double-sized meeting room, or a place outside. Using masking tape, create three squares on the floor or ground arranged in an equilateral triangle. Each square should be able to accommodate one third of the group standing comfortably inside. Arrange the boxes at least twenty feet apart. Next, mark a small X at the midpoint of the triangle equal distance from each of the squares. Place a shoebox or basket containing five or six tokens on the X.

With these arrangements in place, you are now ready to introduce the game. Explain to the youth that they are about to enter the Bermuda Triangle. For those unfamiliar with the Bermuda Triangle, it is an area of the Atlantic Ocean between Bermuda, the Greater

Antilles, and the coast of Florida in which some seventy planes and ships have mysteriously disappeared. Since nobody has been able to explain these mysterious disappearances, many people are afraid to travel to the Bermuda Triangle. Those courageous enough to do so may uncover the secret to one of our planet's greatest mysteries, or, perhaps disappear forever. The risks are real; the opportunities are great. These are your choices in the Bermuda Triangle.

In playing Bermuda Triangle, players are given five tokens each to begin. The winner is the player with the most tokens after all rounds are finished. Each round a different player becomes the tagger. The tagger lives inside the Bermuda Triangle and is responsible for keeping other players from passing through. The triangle is composed of three island safe squares and an abandoned treasure in the middle. All other players begin the round on any of the three safe square islands they choose.

The tagger must protect the triangle, especially the treasure, by tagging any trespassers. The trespasser's goal is to grab a token from the treasure. Only one token may be taken at a time. Any player tagged inside the triangle must give one of his or her tokens to the tagger and return to the nearest safe square. If a player manages to grab a token from the treasure before being tagged, he or she may keep the token but must surrender another as a result of the tag. On the other hand, if a player successfully leaves a safe square, grabs a treasure token, and returns to any safe zone without being tagged, the token is theirs to keep. No tagging is allowed in the safe zones. A player is considered in the safe zone as long as any part of his or her foot is inside the square. Those players losing all their tokens must stay in a safe zone until the next round.

Each round a different youth is chosen as the tagger. Rounds last for two to three minutes or until all the tokens have been taken from the treasure, whichever comes first. Timing of rounds and number of rounds should be tailored to available meeting time. The leader will be timekeeper and referee. Try to allow each youth an opportunity to be the tagger. If time is an issue, consider having two youth be the tagger simultaneously. At the end of each round, award two tokens to all those who left the safe zone. The tagger should also be awarded two tokens. Remember to restock the treasure chest with five or six tokens before starting each round.

Players are not required to leave the safe zone. However, they will soon realize leaving is the only way to get more tokens. At first expect players to be relatively conservative in their attempts at the treasure. This will make for good reflection later. With time, they will discover teamwork can draw the tagger away from the treasure long enough to offer other alert players a better opportunity. When finished, congratulate the player with the most tokens. Recognize all players who left the safe zone. At this point, retire to the reflection area for some well-deserved rest.

Supply List

- ☐ masking tape
- ☐ box or basket
- ☐ watch with a second hand, or stopwatch
- ☐ tokens (pennies or poker chips), about 15 for each youth in the group

Reflection

Read aloud Matthew 17:1–9, Mark 9:2–10, or Luke 9:28b–36.

Questions for Discussion

- ☐ What did the activity have to do with the Gospel, especially transfiguration or conversion?
- ☐ In the activity, why was it risky to leave the safety of the islands?
- ☐ Why was it risky for Jesus and the disciples to leave the mountain? What eventually happened to Jesus in the Gospels?
- ☐ How do you think the disciples and Jesus felt leaving the safe mountain and returning down the mountain where people wanted to crucify Jesus?
- ☐ While Jesus was on the mountain, he was among believers. When we are at church, we are also among believers. We feel safe to speak about God and God's love for us. Why is it difficult to have the same discussions outside of church with non-believers?
- ☐ How do you feel about living Christian values when others around you might not share those values?
- ☐ In the activity, how much risk were you willing to take in order to get the tokens?
- ☐ In life, how much risk are you willing to take in order to bring God's love to others?
- ☐ Jesus and the disciples went up a mountain to pray and get away from things. Where do you go when you need to sort things out?
- ☐ In the activity there were three safe islands. How does a safe and quiet place help you grow closer to God?
- ☐ In the Gospel, Jesus became transfigured before them and appeared dazzling white. How can you tell when someone has been touched by God's love?
- ☐ Why do you suppose Peter wanted to erect tents when Moses and Elijah appeared?
- ☐ What are some ways people try to control God?
- ☐ What things do people hold onto that keep them from growing closer to God?
- ☐ How did the disciples feel when the cloud appeared and spoke?
- ☐ What is it about changing our values and habits that can be scary?
- ☐ In the Gospel, God spoke to them through a cloud. Where do you hear God speaking to you?
- ☐ How does God's word lead you to a stronger relationship with God?
- ☐ What have you discovered from this Gospel and how can you apply it in your life?
- ☐ In the next few days, what risks could you take to respond to God's love?

Catechumenate Connection

This second week of Lent, we are called to a deeper conversion and closer relationship to God. Discuss ways they can become closer to God. How do they feel closer to God when studying Scriptures and praying? How does sharing faith bring them closer to God? What are the risks of being vulnerable when they share their faith with others? What are some of the risks they see themselves facing by living closer to God? What do they feel they must leave behind in order to grow closer to God?

The Catholic Church looks to the saints as examples of how to live closely with God (*Catechism of the Catholic Church* §828, §2030). Catholic tradition recalls stories of many saints who became martyrs by remaining faithful to God despite torture, persecution, and death. Sts. Stephen, Peter, and Paul were all martyred for their faith. Explore how the martyrs took risks and how they were able to have such courage. Who are modern day heroes that risk their reputations and lives for what they believe? What gave Martin Luther King, Nelson Mandela, and Mother Teresa the courage to leave the safety of conformity to speak out against injustices or care for the sick?

As the elect prepare for baptism and catechumens discern baptism, discuss how God's love strengthens them to live their faith. How do they feel about living their faith at home and at school? Who are some of the people whose lives are examples of how to be close to God?

3rd Sunday of Lent (A)

Seeking God ✝ *Discipleship*

Readings

Exodus 17:3–7
Psalm 95:1–2, 6–7, 8–9
Romans 5:1–2, 5–8
John 4:5–42

Theme

Read John 4:5–42. The story of Jesus' encounter with the Samaritan woman is rich with meaning. At first glance the story line seems rather simple: Jesus reveals his identity to a woman who responds by spreading the word to others causing them to believe. The richness comes forth, however, when we look closely at the characters.

Samaritans were looked down upon by the Jews. In fact, a Jew became ritually impure simply by drinking from a vessel handled by a Samaritan woman. Despite this, Jesus reached out to the woman revealing to her something about herself and entrusting to her his identity as the Christ. Why did Jesus choose to bestow such favor upon this woman? We know that she was searching for fulfillment in her life. Her search for water, her life with six different men, her struggle about where to worship, and her expectations of the Messiah speak of her yearning for more in life. Perhaps it was her openness and hunger for meaning, or maybe it was her lowly status as a Samaritan woman that caught his eye. Regardless, she responded to Jesus' promise of eternal life with the zeal of a missionary as she enthusiastically returned to town and spread the story.

We, too, pause this Sunday to reflect upon how earnestly we seek to know God. We consider also our enthusiasm for sharing God's Good News with others.

When exploring the Gospel, help the youth put together a profile of the Samaritan woman. How would they describe the feelings between Jews and Samaritans? What can they deduce about her based on her past, her questions of Jesus, and her actions after speaking with Jesus? Where are some places the youth search for happiness in their life?

Let the youth discuss the significance of Jesus asking a Samaritan woman for water. What do they think this says about Jesus and his regard for all people? How do they suppose the woman felt when Jesus spoke to her? How can they imitate Jesus in this way?

Jesus told the woman his water would become a spring bringing eternal life. What do they suppose this means? How did the encounter change the woman? Let the youth explain

---

how the woman responded to Jesus. Invite them to discuss ways they, too, can share their faith with others.

Activity Summary

The activity is designed to symbolize the experience of the Samaritan woman in the Gospel. Her life of searching, her encounter with Jesus, and her response to his Good News are each paralleled in the activity. The idea is to let the youth discover how God's love and revelation are gifts freely given, how seeking God with an open heart leads to closeness to God, and how sharing God's love with others is a natural response to this love.

The activity begins with the youth working together to find a special envelope. The envelope contains a blue clue that will lead them to a treasure of candy to share among themselves. Each round starts with the leader telling the group where to search for the envelope. Once found, the youth bring the envelope to the leader to be opened. To everyone's disappointment, the envelope will not contain the special clue. After several rounds of unsuccessful searching, the leader will acknowledge how diligently they have been searching and ask the group to state exactly what it is they seek. Responding to their request, the leader will then give the special envelope containing the blue clue to the group. The youth are sure to respond to this good news with a high-spirited dash to the treasure.

Bridging the Activity and Reading

- ☐ Searching for the blue clue represents the Samaritan woman's search for meaning in her life.
- ☐ Once the last false clue is found, the ensuing conversation between the leader and the group symbolizes the conversation between the Samaritan woman and Jesus.
- ☐ The leader giving the group the blue clue signifies Jesus giving the Samaritan woman the gift of living water.
- ☐ Responding to the blue clue by finding the treasure and sharing it among the group represents the Samaritan woman's response to Jesus and her enthusiasm in sharing the Good News with others.

Preparation

Begin by choosing seven to ten different areas to be used during the treasure hunt. These sites need to be large enough to allow the youth to search for envelopes containing clues. If possible, use different parts of the parish facilities to hide the clues. Be careful, however, not to disturb other groups that may be meeting at the same time. If the idea of a large number of youth running through the facility in search of clues seems particularly disruptive, consider using an outdoor area, a gymnasium, the church, or a large gathering room.

Next, prepare a treasure. A basket or bowl filled with enough small, wrapped candy for everyone in the group works well. Also include in the basket a note similar to the following:

You are each very special. You have all shown a wonderful desire to know God. It is a pleasure to be with you as you search for God. Remember, the real treasure is experiencing God's love. What can you do to share the treasure of God's love with others?

Hide this treasure in a secluded location, such as inside a desk or cabinet. The idea is to keep it out of sight from the youth until the very end. Write this location in detail on a blue piece of paper. Fold the paper, place it in an envelope, and keep it with you in a pocket or purse throughout the activity. Be sure the envelope is not visible to the youth until the moment you are ready to give it to them.

Next, identify the locations to hide the envelopes containing false clues. These locations should be widely separated from one another and provide ample places to hide an envelope. Examples of locations may include such sites as the meeting room, the kitchen, outside near the front door, or around the bleachers in the gym. The number of locations will largely dictate the length of the activity. In deciding how many false clues to hide, consider your available meeting time and the space available in your facility. Typically seven to ten is a good number. If in doubt, choose more sites and leave yourself the option of not using all of them if time becomes an issue. Make a list of these locations in the sequence that you will use them during the activity.

Finally, gather an envelope and a blank piece of white paper for each location you choose. Create the false clues by placing a piece of white paper inside each envelope and sealing it. When hiding the envelopes in the chosen locations, be creative in making it a challenge to find each one. The idea is to have the youth search diligently, only to be disappointed when the envelope does not contain a blue piece of paper.

At this point you are ready to introduce the activity. Begin by announcing to the youth that they are about to embark on a treasure hunt. They will be searching for an envelope containing a blue piece of paper. Written on this blue paper are directions that will lead them to a hidden treasure. If they find the treasure, they are free to share it equally among themselves.

Explain to the group that they will be given a hint as to where to search for the envelope. The hint will lead them to a certain area where the clue is hidden. The group will go to the area in an orderly fashion and search as a team. Searching should be done with respect for all property, meaning all items must be handled carefully and neatly returned to their original positions. Once the envelope is found, it must be brought to the leader unopened. Emphasize that only the leader is allowed to open the envelope and determine if the clue is the correct one. If the correct blue clue is not found, the leader will continue offering hints until it is discovered.

When all understand the directions, begin the activity by announcing the general location of the first envelope. Accompany the youth to the site and encourage them to work together as a team. The idea is to let the youth have fun enthusiastically hunting for the clue without letting their zeal turn destructive.

When the first envelope is found, remind them that only the leader can open it. Gather the entire group together, and make a big production of tearing open the envelope and removing the paper inside. When the white paper is revealed, show your disappointment as well. Maintain the youth's interest and enthusiasm by quickly announcing a second location to search for the blue clue envelope. Again, follow the group to this site and supervise the search. Repeat this pattern until either the group finds all of the envelopes, or time dictates the activity should draw to a close.

At this point, gather the youth together and announce that you have three things to tell them. First, tell them you realize how hard they have been searching. The diligence and persistence they showed by continuing to search reveals their determination. Second, tell them you are proud to be the leader of such a fine group of youth. Finally, ask the group to describe exactly what it is they are trying to find. After they answer, announce that you want to give them a special envelope you have been saving for the right moment. Remove the envelope from your pocket or purse, and open it in front of the group. Choose a youth to come forward and read the blue clue. Accompany the youth to the treasure location and share in their celebration once it is found. Be sure to call their attention to the note inside the treasure, asking one of them to read it aloud. After the celebration, move the youth to the reflection site.

Supply List

- [ ] envelopes
- [ ] white pieces of paper
- [ ] one blue piece of paper
- [ ] basket or bowl
- [ ] small, wrapped candy for the entire group
- [ ] note to be placed in the treasure
- [ ] pencil or pen

Reflection

Read aloud John 4:5–42.

Questions for Discussion

- [ ] What did the activity have to do with the Gospel?
- [ ] What does this story tell about the Samaritan woman's past and her hope for the future?
- [ ] What was she searching to find?
- [ ] In the activity, how did you feel each time you found an envelope that did not contain the blue clue?
- [ ] Where do people your age look for happiness in life?
- [ ] How can searching for happiness from popularity, social status, or material possessions be unfulfilling?
- [ ] In the Gospel, how had the woman been trying to find happiness?
- [ ] How do you think the woman felt after each of her marriages ended?
- [ ] How would you describe the feelings between Jews and Samaritans?

- ☐ Why do you think the disciples were surprised to find Jesus speaking with this Samaritan woman?
- ☐ Jesus spoke to the woman even though others would not approve. What does this say about Jesus and his regard for all people?
- ☐ How do you suppose the woman felt when Jesus spoke to her?
- ☐ What are some ways you can reach out to others?
- ☐ Jesus told the woman the water he gives becomes a spring bringing eternal life. What does this mean?
- ☐ What happened in their conversation that caused the woman to believe in Jesus?
- ☐ Why do you suppose Jesus chose to reveal so much to this woman?
- ☐ In the activity, describe your feelings the moment you finally had the blue clue.
- ☐ What did the woman do after her encounter with Jesus?
- ☐ How is this reaction like your reaction when you finally knew the location of the treasure?
- ☐ How do you suppose her life changed after her encounter with Jesus?
- ☐ How can your desires lead you closer to God?
- ☐ Jesus did not condemn the women for her past sins; instead, he treated her with respect and kindness. How can you become more open and less judgmental of others?
- ☐ What are some examples of how you have experienced kindness, forgiveness, or generosity?
- ☐ What have you learned from this Gospel and how can you apply it in your life?
- ☐ In the next few days, what can you do to share your faith and God's love with others?

Catechumenate Connection

This Third Sunday of Lent marks the first of the three-week scrutiny process for the elect. Focus this week on how we as humans thirst for something outside ourselves. Invite the youth to discuss ways people search for more in life. What are some of the things they trust? Which desires and paths lead them away from God? How has their search brought them closer to God? In what areas of their life do they find it difficult to trust God?

In the Gospel, Jesus speaks of the living water that brings eternal life. Ask the youth how they have seen water used in the Catholic Church. Explain the traditional uses of water during Mass, such as making the sign of the cross when entering or leaving the sanctuary, the sprinkling rite, and commingling water and wine during the eucharistic prayer.

Invite the youth to read aloud section 694 from the *Catechism of the Catholic Church* regarding the symbolism of water in Baptism. Discuss the symbolic meaning of baptismal water including the cleansing of original sin, new birth, drinking from one Spirit, and the wellspring of eternal life. Invite the youth to discuss what these images mean to them. Explore any questions they might have regarding baptism.

3rd Sunday of Lent (B)

✝   *Justice*   ✝

Readings

Exodus 20:1–17
Psalm 19:8, 9, 10, 11
1 Corinthians 1:22–25
John 2:13–25

Theme

Read John 2:13–25. The image of Jesus using a whip to drive people from the Temple, turning over tables, spilling coins, and demanding respect for his Father's house is a bit troublesome. Whatever happened to that nice Jesus, the one who made us feel good about ourselves by saying turn the other cheek, love your enemies, and blessed are the meek? The other Jesus was interested in humility; this Jesus, however, is focused on doing justice. Jesus went ballistic witnessing the misuse of power, the misrepresentation of God's will, and the manipulation of the faithful for profit.

Jesus' actions in the Temple say more about the truly Christian response to injustice than could any eloquently phrased sermon. Certainly this anger and energy leaves us a bit uneasy. After all, as followers of Christ are we really called to care so much about the injustices around us, the burdens of the faithful, and the misrepresentation of God that we respond with direct confrontation? It would appear the answer is a resounding *yes*! To care this much requires a deep commitment and union with God. This Third Sunday of Lent we are called to strengthen our union with God and neighbor, and reflect upon our willingness to speak against injustice.

Let the youth explore what gave rise to Jesus' actions in the Temple. How did these people turn worshiping God into financial profit? What was it about selling animals to be sacrificed that bothered Jesus? How did Jesus' understanding of doing God's work differ from that of the Jews? Let them articulate what Jesus must have felt when he witnessed these people's actions. Take the opportunity to discuss injustices the youth experience in their lives. How do they deal with the feelings these injustices bring forth?

In response to Jesus' confrontation, the Jewish leaders demanded an explanation. Jesus responded with a prediction of his death and resurrection. Invite the youth to discuss how Jesus' resurrection was a sign of his authority. Why would Jesus' resurrection convince people he acted in God's name? What other signs might Jesus have performed that convinced people of his union with God? What are some signs today that reveal God's presence?

Activity Summary

The activity this week is designed to let the youth explore injustice, the feelings it can engender, and ways those concerned about justice might respond to such situations. The youth will also be able to discover how Christ was deeply concerned about others and how his relationship with God was much different than what the Jews were teaching at the time.

The youth will be divided into small groups for the activity. Each group will create a skit based on some injustice or manipulation of others that might take place in their lives. They are challenged to include in their skits a third-party character that witnesses the injustice and responds in a way that shows he or she is concerned about justice. Each skit is then performed before the large group and followed by a brief discussion. Those observing the skit are asked to identify the injustice, discuss the feelings it engendered, and explore the just response.

Bridging the Activity and Reading

- ☐ In each skit a just person identifies an unjust or unfair situation. In the same way, Jesus identified an unjust situation when he entered the Temple.
- ☐ In each skit, the just person responds in a way that shows he or she cares about those who are being treated unfairly. Likewise, Jesus in the Gospel responded with direct confrontation to those who were manipulating others.
- ☐ During the discussion the youth imagine what an extremely angry person might do about the situation. The Gospel reading recounts a story in which Jesus became angry about an unfair situation.
- ☐ Imagining how they would feel if they witnessed someone becoming angry about an unjust situation is similar to how the people felt who witnessed Jesus driving the merchants out of the Temple.

Preparation

Preparation for this activity is quite easy. Find a site large enough for groups of three to six youth to perform a simple skit while the rest of the group watches. You might want to arrange chairs in a theater pattern providing ample stage space. A second area will be needed to allow the various groups to meet and develop their skits. Finally, gather pencils and paper to aid the youth in developing their skits.

Before introducing the activity, ask for volunteers from the group to define the terms *manipulate* and *injustice*. After a brief discussion, invite the youth to think quietly about common situations in the typical life of a middle schooler when manipulation or injustice could occur. Next, invite the youth to silently reflect on a circumstance they have encountered where someone has taken advantage of another person or treated someone unfairly.

After a few moments, divide the youth into small groups of three to six. Try not to create more than five groups unless your meeting time is significantly longer than an hour. For large groups, this might require putting more than six youth in each small group. Be sure to place at least one outgoing youth with a strong personality in each group. This youth should be comfortable speaking in front of the large group and confident enough to enjoy the attention of his or her peers. Invite the groups to discuss typical manipulative or unfair situations they have encountered or can imagine.

At this point you are ready to introduce the activity. Announce to the youth that they are about to become actresses and actors. Each group will be given time to create a short skit based on one of the unjust, unfair, or manipulative situations discussed earlier. The skit should portray some manipulative or unjust circumstance. Each skit should also feature a character that witnesses the situation and responds in a way that shows he or she is concerned about acting justly. For example, a skit might show someone in trouble for stealing. The accused person blames an innocent person in order to get out of trouble, but the just person watching the situation speaks out in defense of the innocent person.

Explain that the skits will be performed in front of the large group and each member of the small group should have a role in the skit. After each performance, the audience will have an opportunity to analyze the skit. When everyone understands the directions, distribute paper and pencils, announce the time allotted for rehearsal, and invite them to begin creating their skits.

During the rehearsal time, visit each group to make sure they understand the assignment and stay on task. Be prepared to offer ideas to groups struggling with a story line. They might want to consider situations in which a person is excluded from a group simply because he or she does not wear fashionable clothes or live in an exclusive area of town. Ask the group to consider any incident where a group of people ridicules any other person. Gossip, false accusations, intimidation, and bullying can also be forms of injustice and manipulation.

Some youth may feel uncomfortable performing in front of peers. If such a youth does not warm up to the idea with encouragement, suggest the group place him or her in a non-speaking part or perhaps a role as director of the skit. Every few minutes or so, announce aloud the time remaining for rehearsal.

When the time comes for the performances to begin, ask for a volunteer group to go first. Remind the youth to be a good audience by giving the performers all their attention. After the skit, ask the audience to describe the unfair situation. Invite them to discuss the motives behind the manipulation or injustice. Ask them to consider how they would feel being put in a similar situation. Discuss practical ways they could manage the situation if they were confronted with something similar.

Next, invite them to discuss how the just person acted in the situation. Would they have the courage to speak up if they witnessed the same situation? Lastly, invite them to discuss how the just person would react if he or she became extremely angry about the injustice. How would the youth feel if they witnessed the anger? After the discussion, invite the next group to perform their skit. Again, using similar questions, lead the audience in a discussion about the skit.

After all the performances and discussions, invite the youth to take a few minutes for a social break. Encourage them to stretch, walk around, and talk with each other. Finally, move the group to the reflection site for more discussion.

Supply List

- ☐ paper
- ☐ pencils

Reflection

Read aloud John 2:13–25.

Questions for Discussion

- ☐ What did the skits have to do with the Gospel?
- ☐ In the Gospel reading, who was being manipulated or treated unfairly?
- ☐ Who were the people who received benefits from this unjust situation?
- ☐ Why do you think the Jewish people bought animals to sacrifice to God?
- ☐ Why do you think Jesus became angry with the merchants for implying that people had to buy animals to please God?
- ☐ What do you suppose Jesus believed would please God?
- ☐ What do you think pleases God?
- ☐ How do you think the people felt that could not afford to buy an animal to sacrifice?
- ☐ In your own life, how do you feel when you see someone being treated unfairly?
- ☐ What are some injustices you have experienced?
- ☐ How have you felt being in an unjust situation?
- ☐ How do you deal with your feelings associated with these injustices?
- ☐ Jesus was asked by the Jews for an explanation of his actions, some sign that showed he had authority to act this way. How did Jesus respond?
- ☐ Why would Jesus' resurrection convince people he acted in God's name?
- ☐ What other signs might Jesus have performed that convinced people of his union with God?
- ☐ What are some signs today that reveal God's presence?
- ☐ In this Gospel, how did Jesus describe himself?
- ☐ Why do you think he used the word, "temple?"
- ☐ Do you think Jesus regards all people as temples? Why?
- ☐ How did Jesus feel about the Temple?
- ☐ How do you suppose Jesus feels about the " temples" or people who are unpopular or ridiculed at your school?
- ☐ What are we called to do if we see injustice or manipulation of others?
- ☐ What have you discovered from this Gospel and how can you apply it in your life?
- ☐ In the next few days, how can you stand up against injustice or manipulation of others at school or in your neighborhood?

Catechumenate Connection

Refer to the readings and session for the Third Sunday of Lent (A).

3rd Sunday of Lent (C)

Repentance   ✝   *Conversion*

Readings

Exodus 3:1–8a, 13–15
Psalm 103:1–2, 3–4, 6–7, 8,11
1 Corinthians 10:1–6, 10–12
Luke 13:1–9

Theme

Read Luke 13:1–9. This Third Sunday of Lent the Gospel explores human suffering, our need to repent, and God's patient and forgiving disposition. In response to the people's questions, Jesus establishes that misfortune and suffering are not related to one's guilt. Ours is a God of mercy, not one that delights in punishing sinners. Jesus, however, takes this opportunity to point out the urgency for repentance. His warning implies a spiritual death awaiting those who refuse to repent. The suddenness of death in the two examples alludes to our inability to predict our own death and our need to repent today. The parable of the fig tree speaks of God's patience with humanity. Again, our God is all about mercy and patience.

We are called this Third Sunday of Lent to conversion. To know God is to know mercy, patience, and forgiveness. Our calling is to turn from sin and death, from fear and selfishness, to open ourselves to God's mercy and be re-created again in God's image. Every moment of every day is filled with God's rich love. This Gospel is saying turn toward this wonderful love now, hurry up, jump in, and enjoy the cool water that is God's mercy. Come on, let go of yourself and dive in. God is patiently waiting with open arms.

Let the youth explore why the people asked Jesus about suffering. What assumptions do people today make about God when they see suffering? What do the youth think of Jesus' response? Why do they suppose Jesus warned them to repent or perish? What do the youth think Jesus meant by this?

Jesus follows this discourse with the parable of the fig tree. Invite the youth to discuss whom the fig tree, the gardener, and the owner represent. Let the youth explain the meaning of the parable. What does this parable say about God? How do the youth feel about a God that is patient? Who in their lives have shown them mercy and patience and how have they responded to this?

Activity Summary

This activity allows the youth to recognize a need for urgent change, decide to alter their efforts, and re-create something in a completely different way. The idea is to let the youth explore the dynamics of conversion and repentance. This begins by recognizing and acknowledging a need or weakness and acting upon a desire to change. Conversion requires tearing apart our old perceptions, closely examining our values, and letting God re-create us. This process is a response to God's mercy and patience.

The youth will be divided into small groups or teams for the activity. The teams will compete to be the first to assemble a simple jigsaw puzzle the "right way." The team finishing first will be awarded candy. However, as teams complete their puzzle, they will be told to tear the puzzle apart, place it back in the box, and begin again. Only at this point will they be informed that the "right way" is to assemble the puzzle picture-side-down.

Bridging the Activity and Readings

☐ In the activity the youth recognize a need to quickly re-create their puzzles. In the Gospel, Jesus reminded the people of their urgent need to repent.

☐ In the activity the teams have to change and put their puzzles together in a completely different way. In the parable, the owner wanted the fig tree to completely change and start producing fruit.

☐ After putting the puzzle together the wrong way, each team is given another chance to do it correctly. In the Gospel, God did not cause people to suffer because of their sins. In fact the fig tree was given another opportunity to bring forth fruit.

Preparation

Prepare first by gathering jigsaw puzzles. These puzzles should contain no more than sixty pieces and be extremely easy for youth this age to assemble. One puzzle will be needed for each team. Consider dividing the group into teams of two to six youth each. Prepare your activity space by arranging separate tables for each team in different areas of the room. If tables are not available, clean floor space will work. Award candy is needed for the winning team and consolation candy for the rest of the teams.

Begin by dividing the group into teams of two to six youth. Ask each team to move to a different area of the room so they can concentrate without being distracted. Distribute a puzzle in its box face down to each team with instructions not to touch the box until the contest starts.

Next, explain they are about to compete in a puzzle contest. The members of each team will work together to be the first to complete their puzzle. Whichever team is able to complete their puzzle the right way first, receives award candy. It is essential to pick your words carefully here. In order to have the desired effect, the youth must assume the right way to put the puzzle together is picture-side-up.

To help build enthusiasm, show the youth the award candy. Explain that once the puzzle is completed, each member of the team must raise his or her hand. The leader will then inspect the puzzle. In order to win the prize, the puzzle must pass the leader's inspection. Consolation candy will be awarded to any other team completing a puzzle that passes inspection. Therefore, it is very important that each team complete their puzzle. Once everyone understands, invite the teams to turn over their boxes and begin.

The initial construction of the puzzle should go quickly. You can add to the drama and excitement by walking among the teams telling them how they are doing relative to the others or by giving them encouragement if needed.

When the first team raises their hands to signal their puzzle is finished, quickly go to their table or area and quietly tell them that they did a fine job. Explain, however, they did not put the puzzle together the right way. Tell them they must tear apart the puzzle, and place all the pieces back into the box. Explain that for the purpose of this contest, the right way to put the puzzle together is picture-side-down. The team must now put together the puzzle with all of the pieces facing down. Be ready for the youth to be discouraged. Encourage them by pointing out they are still in the lead, and all the other teams will have to do the same.

As each team completes their puzzle, explain the proper way of completing the puzzle just as you did for the first team. Be sure to encourage the youth, reminding them there are prizes involved for completing their puzzle. You might want to say this is their opportunity to get back in the lead. Remember to make sure each team completely takes apart their puzzle. There will be a strong tendency to keep the pieces together and just flip them upside down.

It is possible that one team might observe another team starting over and inquire about the rules. If this happens, quietly go to this observant team and explain the right way to put together the puzzle. This team should disassemble what they have completed on their puzzle to this point, place the entire puzzle back in the box, and begin assembling it picture-side-down.

This rebuilding of the puzzles picture-side-down will take considerably longer than the original working. Move between the teams offering hints. Suggest they start by putting all the outside pieces together. These border pieces can be recognized by their smooth edges. The corner pieces are also unmistakable. Continue to add to the excitement by updating the teams on their progress relative to the others. Another idea might be to announce a doubling of the award candy. The idea is to create a fever pitch of urgency in the room!

When the first team completes the inverted puzzle, quickly inspect their work and congratulate them. Announce that consolation candy is still available. Immediately divide the youth from the winning team among the other teams and invite them to help. This will keep all the youth engaged in the activity until the very end. Keep doing this with each team that finishes. The remaining teams should readily welcome the extra assistance. Once all the puzzles are completed, reward the first-place team with the top candy and distribute the consolation candy to the others. Finally, move the entire group to the reflection area.

Supply List

☐ simple jigsaw puzzles in their original boxes
☐ first-place candy
☐ consolation candy

Reflection

Read aloud Luke 13:1–9.

Questions for Discussion

- [ ] What did the activity have to do with the Gospel?
- [ ] Why did the people ask Jesus if suffering was the result of being guilty?
- [ ] What do you think people often assume about God when tragedy happens?
- [ ] What does Jesus' response to this question tell us about God?
- [ ] What does the word *repent* mean?
- [ ] In the activity, what did you have to change in order to receive candy?
- [ ] Why did you assume the right way to work the puzzle was face up?
- [ ] What are some examples of situations that are the norms of society that may not be Christian values?
- [ ] How did you feel when you were told to tear apart your puzzle and change your method of assembling it?
- [ ] How do you feel when you realize you must change something about yourself?
- [ ] In the reading, what was required of the fig tree?
- [ ] What do you think the fig tree represents?
- [ ] What does the fact that it was barren represent?
- [ ] What was the gardener's response?
- [ ] Who do you think the patient gardener symbolizes?
- [ ] What did the cultivating and fertilizing by the gardener represent?
- [ ] Why is change so difficult?
- [ ] In the activity, when doing the puzzle picture-side-down, did anyone peek to see what picture was on the other side? Why did you peek?
- [ ] Why is it easy to revert to old ways once we make the decision to change?
- [ ] In the reading, why do you think there is an example of people dying suddenly?
- [ ] Why is it a good idea not to delay repentance and conversion?
- [ ] What things must one leave behind in order to live closer to God?
- [ ] What rewards await us in this life if we have a deeper relationship with God?
- [ ] What have you discovered from this Gospel and how can you apply it in your life?
- [ ] In the next few days, what kinds of perspectives, actions, or attitudes can you change in order to live closer to God?

Catechumenate Connection

Refer to the readings and session for the Third Sunday of Lent (A).

4th Sunday of Lent (A)

Faith   ✝   *Judging Jesus*

Readings

1 Samuel 16:1b, 6–7, 10–13a
Psalm 23:1–3a, 3b–4, 5, 6
Ephesians 5:8–14
John 9:1–41

Theme

Read John 9:1–41. "I came into this world for judgment, so that those who do not see might see, and those who do see might become blind." With these words, Jesus summarizes the point of this Gospel and his mission on earth. It is not so much that Jesus judges us, as it is that we judge him. Truly Jesus was and still is divisive. He simply walked among us speaking of a merciful and loving God and doing wonderful deeds. His message and deeds bothered many people back then just as they bother many today. The question begging to be answered is still the same: How do we judge this Jesus? The blind man judged him to be a prophet, while to the Jewish leaders Jesus was a threat. Does Jesus threaten us, or do we open our hearts to him and live by faith?

John uses blindness on two levels to reveal this truth about Jesus. The blind man was physically blind, begging in the streets, living in need, yet open to others and God. The Pharisees, on the other hand, were powerful in the people's eyes, concerned with maintaining their authority and the law. Jesus restored the blind man's sight. In response, the blind man testified on behalf of Jesus in front of the Jews. After being thrown out of the Temple, he followed Jesus. His was a faith response. His was sight on both a physical and spiritual level. The Pharisees, however, refused to believe. Despite witnessing the results of the miracle, they could not get beyond the fact that it was done on a Sabbath resulting in a violation of the law. They were physically sighted, but spiritually blind.

So, we return to the question: Do we find technical reasons to discount Jesus' teachings? Do we overlook the many miracles before us, focusing instead upon our own agendas? Are we so focused upon success, so self-absorbed that everything is judged solely on how it might benefit us? This Gospel is pleading with us to re-evaluate our lives. We are being called to expand our spiritual sight, to look at the miracles before us, and to respond with open hearts to God's presence. How we answer these questions says much about how we today judge this Jesus.

In exploring the text, let the youth describe how the blind man responded to Jesus. Besides sight, how would they describe the changes in the blind man after meeting Jesus? How would they describe the Pharisees? Why do they suppose the Pharisees refused to believe the blind man? Use this opportunity to discuss why people today find it difficult to follow Jesus.

Let the youth explain why the blind man's parents were afraid to testify on behalf of Jesus. Why was it so important to belong to the Synagogue? What are some examples of how people today are afraid of saying what they really believe? Why do they suppose the healed blind man was willing to testify about Jesus and challenge the Pharisees? What are some ways people can live their faith even when others pressure them to deny it? What are some examples of spiritual sight and spiritual blindness?

Activity Summary

This activity is designed to simulate the two levels of blindness—physical and spiritual—used in the Gospel. Blindfolds will represent physical blindness while running backward will symbolize spiritual blindness. The youth will experience the results of being handicapped and being healed. The idea is to let the activity bridge a discussion about the two types of blindness in this Gospel.

The youth will be divided into two teams and challenged to run two races in relay fashion. In the first race, Team One will be required to run backward representing the Pharisees' spiritual blindness. Team Two will also run backward but do so wearing blindfolds representing the blind man's handicap. The second race is designed to simulate the healing miracle Jesus bestowed upon the blind man. Team One will again run backward, however, this time Team Two will be allowed to run forward naturally without blindfolds. The difference in results should provide a starting place to discuss the Gospel.

Bridging the Activity and Reading

- ☐ Being blindfolded in the activity represents being physically blind in the Gospel.
- ☐ Running backward in the activity symbolizes the Pharisees' spiritual blindness in the Gospel.
- ☐ Removing the blindfold and being allowed to run forward in the activity represents Jesus healing the blind man and the blind man's faith in the Gospel.

Preparation

Preparation begins with choosing an appropriate site for a relay race. A gymnasium, double-sized meeting room, or an area outside works well. Mark a masking tape line approximately three feet in length as a starting line for Team One. Alongside the first line, mark an identical line for Team Two. Next, approximately ten to twenty yards away, mark two identical lines parallel to the starting lines. Each team should now have a starting line and a midpoint line parallel to the starting line. Gather four blindfolds and place two at the starting line and two at the midpoint line for Team Two. During the first relay, only Team Two will be blindfolded.

Begin the activity by dividing the youth into two teams of equal athletic ability. Invite half of each team to move to the starting line, and the other half to move to the midpoint line. Ask the youth to line up single file behind the masking tape lines. Explain that they will be competing in a relay race. The first youth at the starting line will run to the midpoint line and tag the first youth at the midpoint line. That youth will run to the starting line and tag the next youth. This pattern will continue until each team member has had the opportunity to run. The team that finishes first will be the winner.

Explain that each team will be given special challenges during the relays. Team One must run backward during the entire relay. They are, however, allowed to look behind them as they run. If a runner turns to run forward during any part of the relay, he or she must return to the starting point and begin again. Team Two will also run backward during the relay. However, they will have another disadvantage: Team Two will be blindfolded as they run. These runners must rely on the voices of their teammates to direct them to the next runner waiting in line. Explain that two blindfolds have been placed at the starting line and two at the midpoint line so that teammates can prepare the blindfolded runners more quickly. Encourage Team Two to immediately remove the blindfold from the finished runner and quickly place it on a teammate waiting to run. If done efficiently, they should save time and have two blindfolded runners ready.

Expect a great deal of protest from Team Two. Without commenting, invite the first runner at the starting line, and the first runner at the midpoint line to place the blindfold over their eyes. Suggest that they prepare their second runner's blindfolds as well. When the blindfolds are secure, begin the relay.

Cheer for each youth as they run. Be sure to watch for any violations of the rules. As the runners of Team Two finish, be available to help remove the blindfold and place it on the next youth in line.

After the relay, congratulate Team One as the winners. Invite the youth to express any feelings or thoughts they may have had about the fairness of the race. After a few moments of discussion, announce there will be a second relay. Invite the teams to line up as before. Announce that Team One will again run backward during the relay. Team Two, however, will be able to run freely with no handicaps whatsoever. This time, expect protests from Team One. Without comment, begin the relay. When finished, congratulate Team Two for their win.

Supply List

☐ four blindfolds
☐ masking tape

Reflection

Read aloud John 9:1–41.

Questions for Discussion

- ☐ What did the activity have to do with the Gospel?
- ☐ How did you feel being blindfolded and having to run backward in the activity?
- ☐ How do you suppose the blind man in the Gospel felt having to beg on the streets?
- ☐ How did you feel having the blindfolds removed and being allowed to run forward?
- ☐ How do you suppose the blind man felt being healed by Jesus?
- ☐ How did the blind man respond to Jesus after being healed?
- ☐ Besides being healed physically, how else did the blind man change in the Gospel?
- ☐ For Team One, how did you feel when the other team was able to remove the blindfolds and allowed to run forward while your team still had to run backward?
- ☐ Why was it difficult to be happy for Team Two? Why was it easier to focus on your own disadvantage?
- ☐ How do you suppose the Pharisees felt about Jesus?
- ☐ How were the Pharisees' concerns different than the blind man's?
- ☐ Why do you suppose the Pharisees refused to believe the blind man?
- ☐ What are some common everyday miracles that people may overlook in their busy days?
- ☐ What are some concerns or interests people have today that make it difficult for them to follow Jesus?
- ☐ Why were the blind man's parents afraid to testify on behalf of Jesus?
- ☐ Why was it so important to belong to the Synagogue?
- ☐ What are some examples of how people today are afraid of saying what they really believe?
- ☐ How did the Pharisees use intimidation and pressure when interviewing the blind man?
- ☐ Why do you suppose the healed blind man was willing to testify about Jesus and challenge the Pharisees?
- ☐ What are some ways people can live their faith even when it is difficult or they are under pressure to deny it?
- ☐ What are some examples of spiritual sight and spiritual blindness?
- ☐ What have you discovered from this Gospel and how can you apply it in your life?
- ☐ In the next few days, how can your words and actions be a witness of your faith even when others challenge what you believe?

Catechumenate Connection

This Fourth Sunday of Lent marks the second week of the three-week scrutiny process for the elect. Invite the youth to reflect silently on their answers to the following questions: Like the Pharisees in the Gospel, what reasons do you find to not follow Jesus' teachings? What things are most important to you, so important that you would do anything to get or preserve them? Do you judge others based on what they can do for you? What ways are you blinded to God's presence? Like the parents in the story, what makes you afraid to speak the truth? How do you allow others to intimidate you because of your faith? Like the blind man in the Gospel, how have your eyes been opened spiritually? How can you be more open to God's love in your life? How can your words and actions be a witness when others challenge your faith?

Explain to the youth the symbolic meaning of light and darkness in the Easter Vigil celebration. Talk about how the faithful gather in darkness, light the Easter candle, and pass the flame to one another. Describe for them the experience of walking into a dark church with lighted candles and how it feels to have the lights come up. Discuss how light and darkness, sight and blindness are used to illustrate the truth of Jesus' message.

Invite the youth to read sections 1189 and 1192 from the *Catechism of the Catholic Church*. Discuss how Catholics use images to remind them of God's presence and respond accordingly. Invite the youth to think about items they keep in their rooms that remind them of events or people, such as ticket stubs or souvenirs. Ask the youth how mementos help them remember important things in their lives. What things remind them of God's presence?

4th Sunday of Lent (B)

✝   *Faith*   ✝

Readings

2 Chronicles 36:14–16, 19–23
Psalm 137:1–2, 3, 4–5, 6
Ephesians 2:4–10
John 3:14–21

Theme

Read John 3:14–21. Nicodemus, an influential Jewish Pharisee, came to Jesus in the night to learn more. This Gospel passage captures a portion of the response in which Jesus explains his role as the one to be lifted up, the one through whom salvation and eternal life enters the world. He explains how God is not interested in condemning or judging, but in loving and saving the world. Jesus tells Nicodemus it all comes down to faith: either believe and be saved or remain in unbelief and be condemned. Interestingly, Jesus closes his remarks to Nicodemus by using light and darkness to express this truth. Those acting shamefully use darkness to cover their intentions for their hearts are not centered on truth. Those who seek God, however, act in the light so all might see their works.

This Fourth Sunday of Lent we are invited to consider how we, too, might share things in common with Nicodemus. While we also search for truth and seek a closer relationship with Jesus, we are compelled to ask ourselves how often we make that effort under the cover of darkness. What part of our lives do we prefer to keep hidden from others and why? Like Nicodemus, do we find ourselves in positions of responsibility, power or prestige, positions with agendas that make seeking God more difficult? In the end, it is a simple question of faith: Are we courageous enough to believe in Jesus, to open our hearts and expose our actions, our intentions, and our feelings to God and the world, or do we hide these precious things behind a wall of darkness?

In exploring this Gospel, it may be a good idea to provide the youth with background information on Nicodemus from John 3:1–12. Ask the youth why they suppose Nicodemus waited until nightfall to approach Jesus. What do they think the other Jewish leaders would say to Nicodemus if they knew that he was interested in Jesus' teachings? How could this ruin Nicodemus' reputation? How do they think Nicodemus felt about Jesus' remarks regarding those who prefer to act in darkness?

Jesus spoke of how the Son of Man must be lifted up on the cross. How would the youth explain what this means? What do they think is meant by believing in the Son of Man?

Jesus also spoke of God loving the world so much that he sent his Son, not to condemn, but to bring all believers to eternal life. Based on this, how would the youth describe God's feelings for people? How do they think Jesus helps bring people to eternal life? What are some ways the youth see eternal life beginning today? How is not knowing God like being condemned?

Jesus used the images of light and darkness to make a point. Invite the youth to explain what the light and darkness represent. Ask the youth to describe some actions people prefer to hide and why? How would life be different if there were no secrets and everyone's thoughts and actions were visible for everybody to see? Invite the youth to discuss how Christians are called to be honest and open. How does faith require courage?

Activity Summary

This activity explores the experience of concealing one's actions and movements. Soon after beginning, the youth will know the demands concealment and stealth require, how these ways can be enslaving and require total commitment. The idea is to use this experience to let the youth discover why Jesus spoke of evil preferring darkness and truth preferring light. They will be able to contrast this experience with the ease of acting openly and honestly. The ensuing discussion will allow them to explore how faith is a calling to light, openness, and honesty.

The activity is the game Red Light, Green Light. The youth begin by standing side-by-side along a starting line with the leader standing at the opposite end of the area. The object is to be the first youth to touch the leader. When the leader turns his or her back to the group and announces *Green Light*, the youth are free to move toward him or her. However, at any time the leader may announce *Red Light* and quickly turn around. Anyone seen moving even the least bit must return to the starting line and begin again. Play continues until the leader is touched. This version of the game has a surprise ending. Once the leader is touched, it will be announced that the real winners are all those who did not touch the leader.

Bridging the Activity and Reading

- ☐ In the activity, hiding movements from the leader represents Jesus' description of how those who are evil prefer darkness to hide their works.
- ☐ Holding completely still when the leader announces *Red Light* symbolizes how those who disregard Jesus' teachings are frozen in sin.
- ☐ Awarding candy to those whose actions were exposed represents the eternal life Jesus promises for those who believe and live in light.

Preparation

Begin by choosing an appropriate site for the activity. A large grassy area outside is ideal. If one is not available a double-sized meeting room or gymnasium will also work. Next, create a starting line by placing masking tape on the floor or ground. The starting line should be long enough to allow all of the youth to stand comfortably side-by-side.

At this point, you are ready to introduce the activity. Explain to the youth they will be playing a version of Red Light, Green Light. Ask the youth if anyone has played the game and allow those who have to explain the rules to the group. Invite other youth to add any omitted rules until everyone understands the game. Be sure each of the rules outlined in the Activity Summary are included, especially that the first person to touch the leader wins.

Next, begin the activity by inviting the youth to line up, side-by-side behind the starting line. Walk approximately thirty feet from the starting line, face away from the youth, and loudly announce *Green Light*. After a moment or two, announce *Red Light* and quickly turn around. Call out the names of any youth observed moving and send them back to the starting line. Carefully watch the youth for a few extra seconds. Look for anyone to lose their balance or twitch in any way. Quickly call their names and send them back to the starting line as well. When everyone is perfectly still or back at the starting line, turn around and again call out *Green Light*.

Continue this pattern until a youth touches the leader. When finished, call the group together and announce the prize will now be awarded. Distribute candy to all the youth who did not touch the leader. Explain that those who did not touch the leader are the winners in this game. Challenge the youth to listen carefully to the Gospel and see if they can discover why. Invite the youth to move to the reflection site. During the reflection, candy should also be given to the youth who touched the leader for being a good sport.

Supply List

- ☐ candy
- ☐ masking tape

Reflection

Read aloud John 3:1–12, 14–21.

Questions for Discussion

- ☐ What did the activity have to do with the Gospel?
- ☐ In the activity, how difficult was it to hold still when the leader was looking?
- ☐ How can sinful actions be similar to holding still?
- ☐ What did Jesus mean when he talked about evil people preferring darkness?
- ☐ What are some actions people prefer to hide and why?
- ☐ Why do you suppose Nicodemus waited until nightfall to approach Jesus?
- ☐ How do you think Nicodemus felt about Jesus' remarks regarding those who preferred to act in darkness?
- ☐ In the Gospel, Jesus said, "The light came into the world." What did he mean by the light?
- ☐ What did Jesus mean when he talked about truthful people preferring the light?

- ☐ How would life be different if there were no secrets and everyone saw everything people did?
- ☐ What are some ways people can be honest and open about their feelings, actions, and intentions?
- ☐ How does faith require courage?
- ☐ Jesus spoke of how the Son of Man must be lifted up. What does this mean?
- ☐ What does it mean to believe in the Son of Man?
- ☐ Jesus said, "God does not want to condemn us, but give us eternal life." What does this say about how God feels about us?
- ☐ How does Jesus help bring people to eternal life?
- ☐ What are some ways people who are close to God experience eternal life here on earth?
- ☐ How can living without knowing God be similar to being condemned?
- ☐ What have you discovered from this Gospel and how can you apply it in your life?
- ☐ In the next few days, how can your actions show others that you are close to God?

Catechumenate Connection

Refer to the readings and session for the Fourth Sunday of Lent (A).

4th Sunday of Lent (C)

Repentance   ✝   *Forgiveness*

Readings

Joshua 5:9a, 10–12
Psalm 34:2–3, 4–5, 6–7
2 Corinthians 5:17–21
Luke 15:1–3, 11–32

Theme

Read Luke 15:1–3, 11–32. "But now we must celebrate and rejoice, because your brother was dead and has come to life again; he was lost and has been found." These words, unthinkable to the older brother, express the true spirit of God. Ours is a God who longs for us to return, who rejoices in our discovery of him, who runs to meet us with open arms, if we can only muster the courage to face him. The parable of the Prodigal Son eloquently reveals God's heart. It is not judgment, condemnation, or vengeance that God wants. Our weaknesses, impurities, and insecurities are opportunities to experience the wonderful forgiveness and re-union love to be found at the very essence of God's Spirit.

This parable speaks also of our need to repent. Just as the younger son leaves, experiences hunger, and returns to the father, so, too, must we be willing to acknowledge our hunger and return to God. For in this there is much to celebrate. In acknowledging our weaknesses and recognizing the Father's mercy, we come to experience forgiveness and re-union with God. This Fourth Sunday of Lent we are called to a deeper conversion. We pause to reflect on our willingness to acknowledge our hunger and pray for the courage to return to God. We are given a warm image of a compassionate father running to his son, longing to embrace him. Let this image bring forth in us the desire and courage to return to our Father.

This passage begins with the Pharisees commenting on how tax collectors and sinners were gathering around to listen to Jesus. Ask the youth to explain what it was about the Pharisees that prompted Jesus to tell this parable. Let the youth explain whom the younger son, the older son, and the father represent in the parable.

The parable begins with the father giving the younger son his share of the estate. What do the youth think these treasures represent? What are some ways people squander the gifts given to them by God? In the parable, the son gets to the point where he is dying of hunger. What are some examples the youth might give of how living apart from God resembles dying? At this point in the story, the son realizes something about his father. Ask

---

the youth to explain what it is he realizes. Use this opportunity to explore how they realize God's goodness in their lives. The combination of the son's hunger and his memory of his father's goodness cause him to change. Invite the youth to describe the change that happened in the son and what he did in response to this change.

Ask the youth to describe the father's feelings when he saw his son returning. What did the son say to his father upon seeing him? Invite them to discuss how God might feel about us if we return to him in humility. Ask the youth to describe the difference in attitude between the father in the parable and the Pharisees listening to the parable. What message was Jesus trying to send to the Pharisees through the conversation between the older son and the father?

Activity Summary

This activity is designed to roughly parallel the events of the Prodigal Son parable. The idea is to create an experience as a reference for exploring this passage.

The activity begins with a generous distribution of candy. The younger son's departure and return is symbolized by running a relay race. Each youth will run away from their teammates to a midpoint line out of their sight and return as quickly as possible. Despite their efforts, the teams will not be able to run the course in the allotted time and therefore will not qualify for a party afterward. Just as in the parable, a discussion will take place about the team's worthiness for a party. The father's response will be represented in both the teammate's excitement upon the runner's return and in the celebration party after the event.

Bridging the Activity and Reading

☐ Receiving consolation candy before the race symbolizes the father giving the younger son inheritance money.

☐ Running to the midpoint line represents the son's departure, while returning to the starting line represents his return to the father.

☐ The team's failure to meet the allotted time symbolizes the younger son's failure to use his inheritance wisely.

☐ The teammates' excitement as each runner returns represents the father's joy when his son returned.

☐ Being invited to the party despite failing to meet the allotted time symbolizes the father throwing a party for his son despite his son's failure in using his inheritance.

Preparation

Begin by making arrangements for a simple party. Gather party foods, such as cake and punch or chips and soda. Arrange the food and drinks along with paper plates, napkins, and cups on a table in the meeting room. Choose several CDs or tapes the youth would enjoy. Place these next to a boombox on the table. If time allows, create a festive mood in the room by adding crepe paper and balloons.

Next, choose a site for a relay race. An area outside, a large meeting room, or gymnasium works well. During the race, each youth will begin at the starting line, run to a midpoint line, and return to the starting line to tag the next teammate. Using masking tape on the floor or ground, mark a three-foot starting line for each team. Next, choose a place for the midpoint line. This line should not be visible to the youth at the starting line. The idea is to have each runner disappear from his or her teammates' sight for at least ten to fifteen seconds while running the course. As the runners return to tag the next in line, the teammates will be anxiously anticipating their arrival. If the activity takes place outside, consider placing the midpoint line around a corner of a building. If the activity takes place inside, consider having the runner go out of the room and down a hall.

Finally, you will need to determine the allotted time for running the relay. The point is to make the allotted time seem obtainable to the youth, however, in reality the time must be unobtainable. Begin by estimating the time it will take one youth to run the relay. Consider asking a youth of the same age and athletic ability of those in the group to run the relay while timing him or her. Arrive at the estimate by multiplying this time by the number of youth on one team in the activity. You may need to wait until the time of the race in order to determine the actual number of participants on each team. After multiplying the estimated time by the number of youth on one team, subtract one or two minutes from the total. For instance, if it takes a youth thirty seconds to run the course and there are ten youth on each team, three hundred seconds (or five minutes) would be the multiple. Subtract one minute from this total leaving the allotted time at four minutes. This will be the allotted time required for the team to complete the relay. It is very important to accurately estimate the time it will take for the all the youth on a team to run the relay in order to make the allotted time impossible to achieve.

You are now ready to introduce the activity. Lead the youth to the relay site and explain the object of the activity is to run a relay in the allotted time. Each youth will begin at the starting line, run to the midpoint line, touch it, and return to tag the next teammate. Walk the course with the youth so all will know exactly where to run. Announce any team that completes the course in the allotted time will be invited to a party in the meeting room. If a team does not complete the relay in the allotted time, they will receive consolation candy instead. At this point announce the allotted time.

When all understand the rules, divide the youth into teams of equal athletic ability. Invite each team to form a single file line behind their starting line. Give the youth a few minutes to anticipate the start of the race. You might even consider saying the words, *Ready* and *Set*. Instead of saying the word *Go*, invite the youth to relax. Explain that you have decided to give them the consolation candy to enjoy before the race. Tell them you have confidence in each team and feel they will earn that invitation to the party. Distribute candy to the youth and invite them to relax, and enjoy their treat. When they finish, invite them to again line up behind the starting line. This time begin the race.

During the race, make sure each youth touches the midpoint line before returning to the starting line. Consider asking a co-catechist or aide to stand at this line and serve as referee. Encourage the youth by cheering for them by name. Try to create enthusiasm among the teammates so the runners feel the excitement of approaching the finish line. Count down the time by announcing how much time is left every thirty seconds. When the allotted time gets close, add to the drama by counting down the time every ten seconds.

At some point in the relay, the teams will realize it is impossible to complete the race in the allotted time. Continue to encourage them to finish the race; explain that each youth should have the opportunity to run.

When each team has finished the relay, call the youth together. Invite them to share ideas on whom, if anyone, should be invited to the party. After a few minutes of discussion or debate, explain how happy you are that each team had the courage to finish the race when they could have given up. Each person returned to the finish line and that is cause for celebration. Invite them all to the meeting room for a party. After the celebration, invite the youth to the reflection site.

Supply List

- ☐ food for the party, such as cake or chips
- ☐ drinks for the party, such as punch or soda
- ☐ napkins
- ☐ plates
- ☐ forks if needed
- ☐ CDs or tapes
- ☐ boombox
- ☐ masking tape
- ☐ consolation candy
- ☐ stop watch or a watch with a second hand

Reflection

Read aloud Luke 15:1–3, 11–32.

Questions for Discussion

- ☐ What did the activity have to do with the Gospel?
- ☐ What was it about the Pharisees that prompted Jesus to tell this story?
- ☐ Whom do the father, the younger son, and the older son represent in the story?
- ☐ The parable begins with the father giving the younger son his share of the estate. What does this inheritance represent?
- ☐ What are some ways people turn their back on God and squander the gifts given to them?
- ☐ In the parable the son gets to the point where he is dying of hunger. What are some examples of how living apart from God resembles dying?
- ☐ How did you feel when you knew you could not finish the relay in the allotted time?
- ☐ In the Gospel, how do you think the younger son felt when he ran out of money?
- ☐ While he was dying of hunger, what did the son realize about his father?
- ☐ What are some examples of how God shows goodness to you?

☐ In the activity, why was it necessary to change the direction you were running and return to the starting line?

☐ How did the younger son change in the story?

☐ What are some examples of ways we can return to God?

☐ How did the younger son expect his father to react?

☐ How would you describe the father's feelings the moment he saw his son returning?

☐ How do you think God feels when we return to God in humility after we fail?

☐ How do you suppose the younger son felt about his father's forgiveness and the celebration?

☐ In the reading, how did the older brother feel when he found out that his father was throwing a party for the younger brother?

☐ The father and the older son had different attitudes about the younger son's return, just as Jesus and the Pharisees had different attitudes about sinners. How would you describe the differences in these attitudes?

☐ After the race, was there anyone who thought the winning team should be invited to the party? Why?

☐ What does this story say about judging others?

☐ What have you discovered from this Gospel and how can you apply it in your life?

☐ In the next few days, what can you do to respond to God's unconditional love and forgiveness?

Catechumenate Connection

Refer to the readings and session for the Fourth Sunday of Lent (A).

5th Sunday of Lent (A)

Resurrection   ✝   *Faith*

Readings

Ezekiel 37:12–14
Psalm 130:1–2, 3–4, 5–6, 7–8
Romans 8:8–11
John 11:1–45

Theme

Read John 11:1–45. Jesus uses the death of Lazarus to glorify God and increase the faith of those present. On this remarkable occasion, we also see the compassionate side of Jesus deeply troubled, perturbed, and weeping with those he loved at the tomb. The resurrection of Lazarus was perhaps the most astonishing of the many miracles recorded in John's Gospel. Surely Martha, Mary, and the Jews suspected Jesus could have prevented Lazarus' death; after all he had healed and cured many before. But clearly nobody expected Jesus to raise one who had been dead four days. Raising the dead was a feat attributable only to God. And it was precisely this divine power over death that Jesus presented before the people.

Witnessing this resurrection had to profoundly build the faith of those gathered. It showed that Jesus was all about resurrection, all about life, all about making whole again that which was dead. In this way, we see the connection between resurrection and faith: "Jesus told her, 'I am the resurrection and the life; whoever believes in me, even if he dies, will live, and everyone who lives and believes in me will never die. Do you believe this?'" This Fifth Sunday of Lent we, too, ask ourselves the same question Jesus posed to Martha: Do we believe this? In our gut do we know God will prevail over our worries, our concerns, and anxieties? In our heart do we trust God to rebuild us from our broken hearts, our lost dreams, and the many deaths we face each day? Do we look for God to raise us from our tombs, untie us from our burial cloths, and let us go free?

In exploring the text, ask the youth why they think Jesus waited two days before returning to Judea. What risk awaited Jesus in Judea? How do they suppose the disciples felt returning there?

When Martha came out to meet Jesus they discussed the resurrection. Ask the youth if they think Martha expected Jesus to raise Lazarus from the dead that day. Jesus told her, "I am the resurrection and the life; whoever believes in me, even if he dies, will live, and everyone who lives and believes in me will never die." Invite the youth to discuss what Jesus meant by these words. Why did Jesus ask Martha if she believed this?

Mary fell at Jesus' feet weeping. She told him, "Lord, if you had been here, my brother would not have died." He saw the Jews weeping and finally came upon the tomb. Invite the youth to describe how Jesus must have felt throughout all of this. What does Jesus' response reveal about him? Some of the Jews questioned why Jesus could not have done something to prevent this death. Do the youth feel these Jews expected Jesus to raise Lazarus?

Jesus thanked God for hearing him and said, "I know that you always hear me." What does this prayer reveal about Jesus' faith? He continued praying, " ... but because of the crowd here I have said this, that they may believe that you sent me." How did this miracle affect the people gathered that day? What are some ways God touches us with his resurrection power?

Activity Summary

This activity is designed to let the youth experience freedom after being bound to a chair. They will then be able to use their new freedom to help others escape bondage. Observing this unfold will create a wonderful image of how resurrection energy can spread through a community. Additionally, they will subtly be ritualizing the experience of trusting God by physically letting go of those things that bind them. The idea is to let the youth experience bondage, freedom, and trust so they might discover the connection between Jesus' message and spiritual resurrection. The ensuing discussion will invite them to recognize God's resurrection love in their own lives.

The activity begins with the youth seated in chairs in a large circle. Tied to each chair are two bandanas that the youth are not permitted to touch. In the center of the circle is a youth chosen to be the hero. This hero must quickly untie the bandanas from one of the chairs to free that youth. The two of them then carry the bandanas and chair to the center, touch the X on the floor at the center, and then go out to free two more youth. This continues until all the youth are free. The activity is timed and repeated several times to see if they can better their efforts.

Bridging the Activity and Reading

- ☐ Sitting on a chair unable to move represents Lazarus tied and bound in the tomb.
- ☐ The hero running to help symbolizes Jesus coming to Bethany to help his friends.
- ☐ The hero untying the bandanas on the chair symbolizes Jesus raising Lazarus from the tomb.
- ☐ Leaving the chair and bandanas at the center, touching the X, and returning to free others represents how those who came to believe in Jesus that day left their concerns in God's hands and went out to bring God's love to others.

Preparation

Begin by choosing a site for the activity. A large room, a gymnasium, or an area outside works well. Next, prepare the activity area. Using masking tape, make a large X on the floor or ground in the center of the room or outdoor area. Gather enough chairs for each youth (minus one) and place these in a circle around the X. One youth will be designated as the hero and will not need a chair. Arrange the chairs at least ten yards from the X at the center of the circle. Finally, gather two bandanas for each chair. If bandanas are not available, consider using long strips of cloth. Tie one of the bandanas in a loose double knot on the back of each chair and tie the second bandana on a leg of each chair. With these preparations in place, you are now ready to introduce the activity to the group. Explain the object of the activity is to see how quickly they can work together to free everyone in the group. One youth will be designated as the hero and stand at the center of the circle. All others will be seated in the chairs. Each chair will have two bandanas tied to it. The youth in the chairs are considered bound and are not allowed to move as long as the bandanas are tied to their chairs. Only heroes are allowed to touch or untie the bandanas. Everyone else must remain in their chair until a hero unties both bandanas.

When the activity begins, the hero will run to any chair in the circle. He or she will then untie both bandanas from the chair. Once the hero has both bandanas untied, the seated youth will pick up his or her chair and carry it to the center of the circle as fast as possible. At the same time, the hero will carry the bandanas to the center of the circle. The two of them will leave the chair and bandanas at the X.

Explain that the X in the center is kind of a magical place that empowers anyone who touches it to become a hero for one round. Once they have dropped the chair and bandanas, they both must tag the X in the center to become heroes. At this point both youth are heroes and are able to return to free others by untying bandanas. As each youth is untied, he or she will carry the chair to the center while the hero carries the bandanas as was done in the first round. This time all four youth will become heroes by touching the X. This will continue until all youth, bandanas, and chairs are at the X in the center of the circle.

Explain that the leader will time the activity. Challenge the group to free everyone in five minutes or less. Remind them that they are not allowed to move from the chairs in any way until the bandanas are untied. Emphasize that only heroes are allowed to touch the bandanas. No one is allowed to untie or touch the bandanas on their own chair. Also, chairs and bandanas must be placed at the X; sliding or throwing chairs or bandanas is not permitted.

When all understand, choose a hero and begin the game. Watch for violations of any rules. There will almost certainly be a strong tendency to help the hero untie bandanas followed closely by an overwhelming temptation to throw or slide chairs. Be ready to stay on top of these things and remind them to carry their chair as close to the X as possible. Call out the elapsed time every thirty seconds to add to the excitement.

This activity should go very quickly, so consider playing several rounds. After each round, invite the youth to re-create the playing area by placing the chairs in the appropriate places and loosely retying the bandanas on the chairs. Choose a different hero to begin the activity each round. Also, consider adjusting the time of the activity to continually challenge the youth.

Supply List

☐ masking tape
☐ one chair for each youth except the hero
☐ two bandanas or strips of cloth for each chair
☐ stopwatch or watch with a second hand

Reflection

Read aloud John 11:1–45.

Questions for Discussion

☐ What did the activity have to do with the Gospel?
☐ Why did Jesus wait for Lazarus to die before going to Judea?
☐ What risk awaited Jesus in Judea?
☐ How do you suppose the disciples felt returning to Judea knowing the Jews wanted to stone Jesus?
☐ In your own life, why is it often difficult to face people who don't like you?
☐ Martha and Mary both greeted Jesus by saying, "Lord if you had been here, my brother would not have died." Why do you suppose they said this?
☐ Do you think Martha, Mary, or the Jews who were present expected Jesus to raise Lazarus from the dead? Why?
☐ Jesus told Martha, "I am the resurrection and the life; whoever believes in me, even if he dies, will live, and everyone who lives and believes in me will never die." What did Jesus mean by saying he is the resurrection and the life?
☐ What does it mean to live and believe in Jesus?
☐ Why did Jesus ask Martha if she believed this?
☐ How did Jesus feel when he saw Mary and the Jews weeping at the tomb?
☐ Why did Jesus weep?
☐ Jesus thanked God for hearing him and said, "I know that you always hear me." What does this prayer reveal about Jesus' faith?
☐ He continued praying, " … but because of the crowd here I have said this, that they may believe that you sent me." How did this miracle affect the people gathered that day?
☐ What is the last thing Jesus said in the Gospel reading?
☐ How do you think Lazarus felt being freed from his burial clothes?
☐ In your own life, how can worries such as being popular, wearing the right clothes, or having possessions bind you, or keep you from living freely?
☐ In the activity, what did you have to let go of before you could help free others?
☐ In life, what are some things we need to let go of in order to live closer to God?

- ☐ In your own life, have you ever had a day where things were going wrong and then someone did something or said something to make you feel better? Give an example.
- ☐ How was this experience like a resurrection? How did you feel before? How did you feel after?
- ☐ In the activity, how did you feel when you were freed from your chair?
- ☐ How would you describe God's resurrection love and energy?
- ☐ What are some ways you have experienced new energy and new hope in your life?
- ☐ In the activity you were able to free others from their chairs. How was this like bringing God's resurrection energy to others?
- ☐ How can you share God's love with others who are suffering?
- ☐ What have you discovered from this Gospel and how can you apply it in your life?
- ☐ In the next few days, how can you spread God's resurrection energy to others?

Catechumenate Connection

This Fifth Sunday of Lent marks the final week of the three-week scrutiny process for the elect. Invite the youth to reflect silently on their answers to the following questions: When you pray, do you know that God hears you? Do you believe Jesus' message of love leads to resurrection? What are some struggles in your life where you need God's help? How can you be more trusting and open to God's love? What things do you need to let go of in order to grow closer to God? What are some of the ways you have been loved by others? How can you bring God's love to others you meet?

Invite the youth to read section 989 from the *Catechism of the Catholic Church*. Discuss with the youth how they feel about their own resurrection someday. How would they describe the Spirit of God that must dwell within? What teachings of Jesus show them the Spirit of God? What examples of resurrection or renewal in their lives would they like to share? How can they help bring hope and renewed love to others?

Discuss the traditions used in Catholic funerals. Invite them to reflect on why the priest's vestments are often white during a funeral mass. Explain traditions associated with praying for the dead and All Souls Day. Explain how the church believes in the communion of saints, a type of spiritual union that exists between the faithful still living and those faithful who have passed away.

5th Sunday of Lent (B)

Sacrifice   ✝   *Service*

Readings

Jeremiah 31:31–34
Psalm 51:3–4, 12–13, 14–15
Hebrews 5:7–9
John 12:20–33

Theme

Read John 12:20–33. "Amen, amen, I say to you, unless a grain of wheat falls to the ground and dies, it remains just a grain of wheat; but if it dies, it produces much fruit." Jesus used this symbolism to capture not only the truth of his life on earth, but to communicate something of the spiritual life awaiting all who would follow him. While we are all naturally drawn to the good energy of life, the eating, laughing, and playing that makes it so enjoyable, we are reminded here that true spiritual life demands that we sacrifice our will for the service of others.

Spirituality is not about preserving one's own life nor is it about being served. Instead, Jesus calls us to surrender our self-interest and serve others if we are to live in God's love. Real death is a very troubling thing. Jesus was troubled over the death that awaited him, yet he embraced it to glorify God. We, too, are called this Fifth Sunday of Lent to face the death to which we are called. A life centered on the needs of others requires a certain death to one's self. The demands of such a life are not glamorous. Yet, the real spirit of love is focused upon the well being of others. When we trust love and let it fill our hearts, we work with God to bring more love into the world. This abundant love is the wonderful fruit born of the grain's death.

In the Gospel, Jesus does not meet with the Greeks who requested a visit with him. Invite the youth to discuss what Jesus was focused upon at this time. Ask the youth what Jesus was referring to when he said a grain of wheat must die in order to produce much fruit. How does this saying apply to our spiritual life? What are some ways people die to their desires and needs in order to help others? Jesus talks about loving and hating one's own life. Discuss with the youth what Jesus meant by this. What does it mean to serve Jesus?

In the second part of the reading, Jesus is troubled. Discuss with the youth the feelings Jesus must have experienced the days before his crucifixion. How do they feel at times when they anticipate something difficult? Ask them how Jesus' death and resurrection

---

glorified God's name. Invite the youth to discuss what it must have been like to hear the voice from heaven. What are some signs of God's presence today?

Jesus spoke of drawing everyone to himself after his resurrection. Invite the youth to discuss what this means. How does God's love draw people together? How do we experience God's love through others?

Activity Summary

The youth will work together in this activity to bake a large cookie. Each youth will be given an ingredient that he or she must sacrifice into the mixing bowl. While the cookie is baking, the youth will reflect upon the activity and Scriptures. When finished they will share the cookie together.

The idea of this activity is to let the youth experience sacrifice for the greater good. In giving up their ingredient and tasting the good cookie born of the sacrifice, they will have a rich perspective from which to reflect upon the Gospel. Gathering together to share the cookie will symbolize Jesus drawing everyone to himself upon his resurrection.

Bridging the Activity and Reading

☐   Sacrificing the ingredient in the activity symbolizes the death of a grain of wheat in the Gospel.

☐   The cookie created from all the sacrificed ingredients represents the fruit produced by the death of a grain of wheat.

☐   Gathering together to share the cookie symbolizes Jesus drawing everyone to himself after his resurrection.

Preparation

Four steps are required to prepare for this activity. First, before the session begins, make arrangements to use a kitchen facility with an oven. Second, gather the cookie ingredients and utensils from the supply list following this section. If possible, gather enough utensils so that each youth can have their own measuring cup or spoon. The idea is to let each youth have a measured ingredient in his or her possession before the mixing begins. Third, to facilitate the actual preparation of the cookie, copy the recipe on a poster board. The fourth step helps prepare for the distribution of the nine ingredients among the group.

For groups with nine or fewer youth, simply write each ingredient and its quantity from the list onto separate slips of paper. These slips will be distributed to the youth at the beginning of the activity. For groups with more than nine youth, consider giving the same ingredient to more than one youth. For example, three youth could be given flour; two could be given one cup and the third could be given one-fourth cup. However you decide to divide the ingredients, be sure to record the quantity and type of ingredient to be given to each youth on a slip of paper. Also be sure the combined quantity of an ingredient on each slip of paper equals the amount needed in the recipe. It will not matter if some youth have a larger amount of an ingredient than others, nor will it matter if some youth have more than one ingredient.

With these preparations in place, you are now ready to introduce the activity to the group. Announce that preparations have been made to allow the group to bake a large cookie to be shared at the end of the session. Explain that each youth will be given an ingredient needed for the cookie. It will be necessary for each person to sacrifice his or her ingredient into the mixing bowl in order to make this work. Before moving into the kitchen, ask the youth if they are willing to sacrifice their ingredient. Although it should be easy to get the entire group to agree, make a big deal of asking each youth individually. After all agree, take a moment to emphasize the need for safety while baking, and move to the kitchen.

Randomly distribute the prepared slips of paper. If the slips cannot be evenly divided, give some youth more than one. Next, invite each youth to choose the appropriate ingredient and utensil and measure his or her ingredient if applicable. Whoever adds the vanilla should hold the bottle of vanilla and measure it just before adding the ingredient. Next, direct the youth's attention to the poster board. Invite the youth with the margarine to place it in the bowl. Proceed in sequential order until all the ingredients are added. Chose a different youth to mix the cookie batter after each ingredient is added.

When the cookie is placed in the oven, move to the reflection area. Make sure to keep an eye on the time. When the cookie is finished, return to the kitchen and remove it from the oven. Allow the cookie to cool for a few minutes, slice and enjoy it with the youth. If the reflection portion of the session is not finished, consider continuing the discussion in the kitchen while enjoying the treat.

If a kitchen facility is not available during the session time, consider substituting a punch recipe for the cookie recipe. Divide the liquid ingredients into containers before the session and distribute to the group. Allow each youth to add his or her ingredient into a large punch bowl.

Supply List

Ingredients
- ☐ 2 ¼ cup of flour
- ☐ 1 teaspoon of baking soda
- ☐ 1 teaspoon of salt
- ☐ 1 cup of butter
- ☐ ¾ cup of sugar
- ☐ ¾ cup of brown sugar
- ☐ 1 teaspoon of vanilla
- ☐ 2 eggs
- ☐ a 12-ounce package of chocolate chips

Utensils
- ☐ one large bowl
- ☐ one 10 x 13 pan
- ☐ one hand-held mixer

- ☐ one spatula
- ☐ cooking spray
- ☐ one timer
- ☐ measuring cups
- ☐ measuring teaspoons
- ☐ prepared poster board
- ☐ amounts of ingredients written on slips of paper to distribute to the youth

Recipe

Preheat the oven to 375°. Spray the pan with cooking spray. Place the margarine in the bowl. Mix the margarine until smooth. Add the sugars and beat until smooth. Add eggs, one at a time. Next, add vanilla, baking soda, and salt. Add flour. Add chocolate chips and mix with a spatula. Pour mixture into prepared pan. Bake in oven approximately 20 minutes. Cool for 10 minutes.

Reflection

Read aloud John 12:20–33.

Questions for Discussion

- ☐ What did the activity have to do with the Gospel?
- ☐ In the activity, what were you asked to do before you went into the kitchen?
- ☐ What would have happened if you had kept your ingredient to yourself?
- ☐ In a sense, your ingredient had to die, or become something else in order to make a cookie. How is that like a grain of wheat dying to make a plant?
- ☐ What was Jesus referring to when he said a grain of wheat must die in order to produce much fruit?
- ☐ How does this saying apply to our spiritual life?
- ☐ Why do you often have to die to your own wants and desires in order to help others?
- ☐ In the activity, was it better to eat the cookie, or would it have been better to eat all the ingredients separately? Why?
- ☐ Which has more potential in farming, one grain of wheat, or a plant that can produce many grains of wheat? Why?
- ☐ What does selfishness and not sharing your cookie ingredient have in common?
- ☐ What are some ways people can be like the grain of wheat that refuses to die?
- ☐ How is helping others similar to putting your cookie ingredient into the mixing bowl?
- ☐ What are some ways people can be like the grain of wheat that dies in order to bring more life?
- ☐ What are some examples of ways that you put others' interests before your own?
- ☐ How is this like serving and following Jesus?
- ☐ In the reading, Jesus says, "Whoever serves me must follow me, and where I am, there also will my servant be." What do you think this means?

- ☐ What does it mean to serve Jesus?
- ☐ If we follow this teaching, how must we die to ourselves?
- ☐ In the Gospel, why do you think Jesus was troubled?
- ☐ What feelings do you suppose Jesus experienced the days before his crucifixion?
- ☐ How do you feel when you anticipate a situation that will be difficult?
- ☐ What would Jesus do to glorify God?
- ☐ What do you suppose it was like to hear the voice from heaven?
- ☐ What are some signs of God's presence today?
- ☐ In the reading, Jesus says, "And when I am lifted up from the earth, I will draw everyone to myself." What do you think this means?
- ☐ How does God's love draw people together?
- ☐ How are you drawn to Jesus?
- ☐ How do we experience God's love through others?
- ☐ What have you discovered from this Gospel and how can you apply it in your life?
- ☐ In the next few days, how can you die to yourself and be fruitful for God?

Catechumenate Connection

Refer to the readings and session for the Fifth Sunday of Lent (A).

5th Sunday of Lent (C)

✝   *Forgiveness*   ✝

Readings

Isaiah 43:16–21
Psalm 126:1–2, 2–3, 4–5, 6
Philippians 3:8–14
John 8:1–11

Theme

Read John 8:1–11. This Fifth Sunday of Lent marks the third consecutive week we hear of God's mercy and forgiveness. This wonderful story tells of Jesus' willingness to forgive, his compassion for the woman, and his ability to rise above the narrow precepts of the day. While the Pharisees cleverly force Jesus to choose between the woman's life and maintaining the law, Jesus responds with a surprising third option. He challenges them to look within and recognize their own weaknesses and need for forgiveness. Looking at the woman's actions in light of their own shortcomings gives the Pharisees the needed insight to extend mercy to the woman.

We, too, take this opportunity to look within ourselves. How quick are we to judge and condemn others? How do we throw stones with our words and actions at those who are weak? Like the woman, how do we need to be forgiven and accepted unconditionally by others? This episode reminds us that Jesus is not so much concerned about condemning our weaknesses as he is about making us whole again. We would do well to extend this same mercy to others, for who among us is really without sin?

In exploring the text, invite the youth to discuss the difference between how the Pharisees and Jesus felt about the woman. What were the Pharisees most concerned about? What was Jesus most concerned about? How would the youth describe the Pharisees' real intentions?

The woman was brought before everyone and made to stand in the middle while the Pharisees announced what she had done. How do the youth suppose this woman felt? How do the youth suppose people feel when others bring attention to their shortcomings? The Pharisees wanted to kill the woman. How do the youth feel when others want to harm them?

Jesus responded to the Pharisees by saying, "Let the one among you who is without sin be the first to throw a stone at her." Ask the youth to explain why Jesus said this. What do they suppose Jesus wrote on the ground? Why would the Pharisees begin walking away in response to what Jesus had written? Have the youth ever had a similar situation when they have been more forgiving with others after being reminded of their own shortcomings?

Jesus told the woman he did not condemn her. How do they suppose the woman felt hearing this? What are some examples of how the youth have experienced forgiveness? How did they feel being forgiven?

Activity Summary

This activity is designed to let the youth experience two responses toward transgressions, punishment, and forgiveness. The idea is to let them discover how the Pharisees' and Jesus' response to sin differed. Experiencing the difference in these two responses will also provide them the perspective to better understand the effect forgiveness has on the community.

The activity is twofold and consists of two different versions of the game, tag. The first version will require players to leave the game and stand in a designated area as soon as they are tagged. This one-chance version is designed to represent the Pharisees' desire to judge and condemn others when they sin. After several rounds, the youth will then begin playing a second version of tag. This forgiveness version resembles freeze tag and represents the mercy Jesus extended to the woman. When a youth is tagged, he or she is still in the game but must stand frozen until touched by a free teammate. Once touched by a teammate, he or she is free to run again.

Bridging the Activity and Reading

- ☐ In both games, being tagged symbolizes the woman's sin.
- ☐ In the first tag game, the punishment for being tagged is immediate removal for the rest of the game. This represents the old law of the Pharisees and their desire to punish the woman.
- ☐ Standing in the penalty box symbolizes the woman standing in the middle of the Temple area.
- ☐ In the freeze tag game, being unfrozen by another runner and free to run again represents Jesus' willingness to forgive the woman and set her free.

Preparation

Begin by choosing a site for the activity. A large area outside or gymnasium will work well. Next, using masking tape or cones, mark boundaries for the playing area. The area should have ample room for the youth to run while keeping them in sight of the leader. Typically a square thirty yards on each side will be sufficient. Next, create a penalty box for tagged runners. Mark with masking tape a rectangular area outside the playing boundaries large enough for all the youth to stand comfortably. It should be close enough to the playing area to allow the youth standing within to watch the game.

Introduce the activity by announcing they will be playing a version of tag. Certain players will be taggers; the others will be runners. Once a runner is tagged, he or she must immediately leave the game and stand in the penalty box. The idea is to avoid being tagged as long as possible. All players must stay inside the playing boundaries during the game. Anyone stepping across a boundary line will be sent to the penalty box. At this point, walk the boundaries with the youth. When all understand the rules, choose the appropriate number of taggers and begin the game. The number of taggers will be determined by the number of youth playing the game. Plan on having a five to one ratio, that is, one tagger for every five runners.

The game should go quickly. Consider playing the game several times choosing different youth as the taggers each time. At the end of the last game, invite all the youth to the penalty box. Discuss the rules of the game and ask if they felt it was fair or unfair. How could the game be more fair for the runners?

After the discussion, announce to the youth they will be playing a different game. This game will be a version of freeze tag. Explain that in this version, if a tagger touches a runner, he or she is frozen and unable to move, but remains in the game and can shout to another runner for help. Any runner who is not frozen can touch any frozen runner and set him or her free. Play continues until all runners are frozen or the leader stops the game due to time.

When all understand, begin the game. After a few minutes of play, stop the game and choose new taggers. Consider varying the number of taggers to make the game more challenging for the taggers. After enough time has passed, move the youth to the reflection site for some well-deserved rest.

Supply List

☐ masking tape

Reflection

Read aloud John 8:1–11.

Questions for Discussion

☐ What did the activity have to do with the Gospel?
☐ In the Gospel, Jesus was quietly sitting and teaching people. Why do you think the Pharisees brought the woman to him?
☐ What were the Pharisees most concerned about?
☐ What was Jesus most concerned about?
☐ What was different about how the Pharisees and how Jesus felt about the woman?
☐ How do you think the woman felt when her sin was announced before the crowd?
☐ How did you feel in the first version of tag when you were forced to leave the game?
☐ Have you ever been caught doing something wrong and others found out about it? Give an example.
☐ How did you feel in that situation?
☐ How do you suppose people feel when others bring attention to their shortcomings?
☐ The Pharisees wanted to kill the woman. How do you feel when others want to harm you?

☐ In the first version of tag, it would have been impossible to remain untagged forever. How was your inability to remain untagged similar to our inability to avoid sin?

☐ Jesus responded to the Pharisees by saying, "Let the one among you who is without sin be the first to throw a stone at her." Why did Jesus say this?

☐ What do you think Jesus wrote in the sand?

☐ Why did the Pharisees begin walking away in response to what Jesus had written?

☐ Can anyone describe a time when you saw someone who became less critical of another person after he or she was reminded of his or her own weaknesses?

☐ How do you suppose the Pharisees felt as they left the scene reminded of their own sins?

☐ How do you think the woman felt when all the Pharisees left and Jesus forgave her?

☐ In freeze tag, how did you feel being touched by a teammate and allowed to run again?

☐ What are some examples of how people have forgiven you?

☐ How did you feel being forgiven?

☐ What does the sacrament of reconciliation have to do with forgiveness and freedom?

☐ What have you discovered from this Gospel and how can you apply it in your life?

☐ In the next few days, how can you become more understanding, more patient, more accepting, or more forgiving of those who offend you?

Catechumenate Connection

Refer to the readings and session for the Fifth Sunday of Lent (A).

Palm Sunday (ABC)

✝   *Christ's Passion*   ✝

Readings

Isaiah 50:4–7		
Psalm 22:8–9, 17–18, 19–20, 23–24		
Philippians 2:6–11		
A: Matthew 26:14—27:66	B: Mark 14:1—15:47	C: Luke 22:14—23:56

Theme

Read Luke 22:14–23:56. Palm Sunday, also known as Passion Sunday, begins with Jesus triumphantly returning to Jerusalem on the back of a colt. This opening image is one of majesty and love for the Beloved Master in the midst of his people. Before the week ends, however, this wonderful image is replaced with Jesus' passion, crucifixion, and death. Those loving multitudes, along with the disciples proclaiming Jesus' praise soon abandon him. This final week of Lent, we retell the culmination of Jesus' ministry and life on earth. We revisit the agony of death in order to prepare for the miracle of resurrection.

While the readings and Psalm always remain the same for Palm Sunday, each year a different passion narrative is read. The activity outlined here uses Luke's Passion account.

Reading the Passion story is in itself an experience of death energy. The detailed accounts of betrayal and agony, of humility and abandonment, of injustice and death lead the reader into a deep communion with Jesus' suffering. It is precisely this suffering, this death energy, this darkness of the soul that gives meaning to Christ's life. Let the youth discover how resurrection requires death. Help them explore their own suffering and sacrifice. How does Jesus' suffering help them with their own struggles?

As the youth reflect upon the events of Jesus' passion, encourage them to express how they feel about what happened. Look for opportunities to bridge between these events and events of their own lives. How do they deal with injustice and suffering? What images from the Passion narrative have special meaning to them?

Activity Summary

This activity is designed to explore the Passion narrative in a stations' format. Ten passages from Luke's Gospel with visual aids, discussion questions, and reflection questions are provided. Each station will center the youth's attention around a theme-based image as a passage is read. Discussion questions will guide the youth to discover the text and bridge

---

it to their lives. Reflection questions are also provided at the end of each discussion. These questions are to be reflected upon in silence, not discussed. Movement is designed between the stations to facilitate attention.

Preparation

Preparation consists of collecting the visual aids in the supply list that follows this section. Choose a quiet, prayerful site with ample space to conduct the activity; the church or a side chapel is ideal. Place these images evenly throughout the space in the order they are listed. Be sure to leave enough room to allow the group to get up and move a short distance between each station. Consider arranging adequate and comfortable seating around each image to facilitate visibility and discussion. Finally, mark or highlight the ten readings in Luke's Gospel.

With these preparations in place, you are now ready to begin. Once the youth gather, briefly explain the format of the activity and invite them to move to the prepared area. Begin each station with the leader reading the Gospel passage. Be sure to plan your discussion time based on the available time for your period. A six-minute allotment for each station will take one hour. Keep the reflection on the last question of each station to about thirty seconds before moving onto the next station.

Remember the idea is to provide the youth an opportunity to explore the Passion while reflecting upon its meaning in their own lives. Naturally, this activity will be somewhat different than others. Therefore, it will be important to keep the group moving on schedule without rushing. Consider ways to create a prayerful environment, balanced with movement, at a pace that will hold the youth's attention.

Supply List

- ☐ Gospel readings

Images
- ☐ plate and cup
- ☐ trophy or a picture of a trophy
- ☐ prayer book
- ☐ Hershey's Kisses
- ☐ plastic knife
- ☐ Halloween mask
- ☐ mouse trap
- ☐ crown
- ☐ eraser
- ☐ egg
- ☐ seed

Stations with Questions for Discussion and Reflection

Station 1: Jesus eats the Last Supper with his disciples.
> Luke 22:14–20
> Visual aid: plate and cup to represent the Last Supper

☐ Why do you think Jesus told his disciples to remember him and his sacrifice by sharing bread?

☐ How can remembering Jesus, his sacrifice, and his message help you grow closer to God?

☐ Jesus spoke of the cup as the new covenant in his blood. What is a covenant? What does Jesus ask us to do in order to be more like him?

☐ What sacrifices are required of you in order to live closer to God?

Reflection: When do you find it difficult to remember Jesus' sacrifice and his message of love? How can remembering God's love help you in difficult times?

Station 2: The disciples argue about who will be the greatest.
> Luke 22:24–30
> Visual aid: trophy or a picture of a trophy to represent being the greatest

☐ Why do you suppose the disciples were arguing over who was the greatest?

☐ How do you suppose they felt when Jesus told them the greatest should be the servant of all?

☐ How do people act when they are concerned only about being the greatest or best?

☐ What are some ways you can be humble and serve others?

Reflection: When do you try to be better than others? How do you feel about yourself and others at these times?

Station 3: Jesus prays in the garden.
> Luke 22:39–46
> Visual aid: prayer book to represent Jesus praying in the garden

☐ What do you suppose Jesus was feeling as he prayed in the garden and his sweat became like blood?

☐ What did Jesus mean when he asked the Father to take the cup away from him?

☐ Why do you suppose Jesus prayed, "not my will but yours be done?"

☐ How does trusting God help you deal with difficult things in your life?

Reflection: When do you avoid doing the right thing because it is difficult? How can Jesus' example help give you courage to do the right thing?

Station 4: Judas betrays Jesus.

    Luke 22:47–53

    Visual aids: Hershey's Kisses to represent the kiss of betrayal, plastic knife to represent a stab in the back

- [ ] Why do you think Judas betrayed Jesus?
- [ ] How does it feel to be betrayed or punished for something you did not do?
- [ ] Why did Jesus not want the disciples to use violence to protect him?
- [ ] What are some Christian ways to respond to those who hurt you?

    Reflection: What are some ways you betray others with your actions and words? How can you become more patient with those who offend you?

Station 5: Peter denies Jesus.

    Luke 22:33–34, 54–62

    Visual aid: Halloween mask to represent Peter hiding his identity

- [ ] What happened to make Peter go from courageously supporting Jesus unto death to denying him three times?
- [ ] When is it easy to follow Christ and when is it difficult?
- [ ] How does fear keep us from acting with love toward others?
- [ ] How do you suppose Peter felt when Jesus looked at him after the cock's crow and he realized he had denied Jesus?

    Reflection: What are some things you feel very sorry for having done? How can you avoid these things in the future?

Station 6: Jesus talks to the Sanhedrin.

    Luke 22:66–71

    Visual aid: a mousetrap to represent how the Sanhedrin was trying to trap Jesus

- [ ] Why do you suppose the Jewish religious leaders asked Jesus if he was the Messiah?
- [ ] Why were they trying to trap Jesus?
- [ ] How does judging others create prejudice?
- [ ] How do people treat others they have judged as bad?

    Reflection: In your heart, who have you judged to be unworthy? What can you do to accept others as they are?

Station 7: Jesus is before Pilate and Herod.

Luke 23:13–25

Visual aid: a crown to represent Jesus before the rulers

☐ How do you suppose Jesus felt when the crowd shouted for him to be crucified even though everyone knew he was innocent?

☐ How do you respond when people treat you unjustly?

☐ Why do you suppose Pilate gave into the demands of the crowd and let them crucify Jesus?

☐ What are some examples of how peer pressure affects you and your friends?

Reflection: When have you given into the crowd and not done the right thing because it was unpopular? How can you respond to peer pressure with courage?

Station 8: Jesus is crucified.

Luke 23:33–38

Visual aid: an eraser to represent forgiveness

☐ How was Jesus able to forgive those who were crucifying him?

☐ What would happen if you were able to always forgive others who offended you?

☐ How did you feel when you heard what the rulers and soldiers said to Jesus as he was being crucified?

☐ Why is it difficult to respond to hurtful words with kindness?

Reflection: How do your words bring suffering to others? How can you become more sensitive to how others feel?

Station 9: Jesus assures the criminal.

Luke 23:39–43

Visual aid: an egg to represent a new beginning for the criminal

☐ What happened inside the second criminal that caused him to speak out on behalf of Jesus?

☐ Why do you suppose the second criminal had a change of heart?

☐ Why do you suppose the second criminal saw Jesus differently than those who crucified him?

☐ How does your attitude change when you are in need?

Reflection: What would you change about yourself if you knew that, like the criminal, it was your last chance? What change would help you see things differently and help you become more understanding?

Station 10: Jesus dies.

Luke 23:44–49

Visual aid: a seed to represent changing to new life

☐   What do Jesus' last words say about the relationship he had with God?

☐   Why do you suppose the centurion believed in Jesus' innocence?

☐   How do you suppose those who witnessed Jesus' crucifixion felt once Jesus died?

☐   What are some of the most difficult times you have faced in your life?

Reflection: When have you felt the most sadness or pain in your life? How do you feel knowing Jesus suffered and died, but that it was not the end?

Catechumenate Connection

Holy Week represents the final week of preparation for the elect before their baptism at the Easter Vigil. Explore how they feel about their upcoming baptism. What sort of changes have they experienced on this faith journey? What questions or concerns do they have on this final week? What images from Christ's passion seem to have particular meaning for them?

For the catechumens and the elect, reflect upon the suffering and hardships Jesus faced on the way to crucifixion. How do they feel about taking on suffering and hardships as a follower of Christ? How does Jesus' response to suffering help them handle the difficulties in their own lives? What areas of their own life do they feel a need to surrender more to God?

Discuss how Catholic tradition uses various images to remind people of Christ's suffering. Explain the Stations of the Cross, and how this devotion is often prayed during Lent. While it is natural to be drawn to energy such as that of the resurrection, we always remember how suffering and death is a part of our life experience. Explore some of the images Catholics use to remember Christ's suffering. Explore also how Christians are called to minister to those who are suffering, hungry, oppressed, and treated unjustly.

Part 2: Easter

Easter Sunday (ABC)

Resurrection	✝	*Faith*

Readings

The Mass of Easter Day
Acts 10:34a, 37–43
Psalm 118:1–2, 16–17, 22–23
Colossians 3:1–4 or Corinthians 5:6b–8
John 20:1–9

Note the Easter celebration begins on Saturday evening with the Easter Vigil Mass. This highest feast of the year celebrates the victory of light over darkness and welcomes the elect into full communion with the church through baptism. Nine readings recount our salvation history on this night, culminating with Luke's account of the resurrection (Luke 24:1–12.) The Mass of Easter Day, celebrated the next morning, uses the readings listed above. Two options are provided for the second reading. If Easter Mass is celebrated in the afternoon or evening, the Gospel account of the disciples on the road to Emmaus (Luke 24:13–35) may be used in place of John 20:1–9. Additionally, the Easter Vigil Gospel (Luke 24:1–12) may be substituted at any of these Masses. Be aware of these options as you prepare your session plan as youth may attend different Masses. The activity planned for this session, however, will work with each of the Gospel readings.

Theme

Read John 20:1–9. Everything changes with Jesus' resurrection on Easter morning. All that Jesus stood for, from turn the other cheek to love your neighbor as yourself, is affirmed with his resurrection. For us, it means those times we are in the grip of death's energy—times when we are lonely, broken, mournful, ridiculed, or persecuted—are opportunities for God to bring forth life's energy with transforming power. Death is no longer the victor. We are now empowered to face death with the hope of resurrection, to respond to offenses with forgiveness, to return hate with love, and to touch suffering with compassion.

This all started when Mary of Magdala found the tomb empty early that Sunday morning. Not understanding what had happened, Mary ran to tell the disciples what she had found. Here is a good opportunity for the youth to reflect upon how they react to amazing and unexpected news. How would they have felt if they were in Mary's shoes that morning?

Mary thought someone had taken Jesus from the tomb. Hearing this, Peter and the other disciple raced to the tomb. Invite the youth to discuss how the two disciples must have felt hearing Mary's news. The disciples wanted to see the tomb for themselves. How do the youth discern if what others tell them is true?

When the beloved disciple went into the tomb and discovered the burial clothes and the rolled-up head cloth but no Jesus, he believed. How do the youth use their eyesight to experience God? Lead the youth to discover other ways they can see spiritually beyond their physical senses. How do they know in their hearts that Jesus' message is true? What is the evidence of resurrection in their world? In their own words, how would they describe how Jesus' resurrection changed things?

Activity Summary

The objective of this activity is to explore the experiences of the disciples and Mary of Magdala on Easter morning. The youth will work together to earn clues to guide them to a treasure. Following the clues, they will discover the treasure is not where they expected. Like the disciples, they will need to piece together the new evidence to find the treasure. Once found, they are commissioned to share it with others. Encourage them to discover the various layers of meaning during the reflection.

Bridging the Activity and Reading

☐ The treasure symbolizes Jesus. The church (or side chapel) represents the tomb.

☐ The relay race represents how the disciples raced to the tomb on Easter morning.

☐ The search for the treasure represents the disciples looking for Jesus on Easter morning.

☐ The youth's surprise at not finding the treasure in church symbolizes the surprise of Mary and the disciples when they found an empty tomb.

☐ The note inviting the group to share the candy symbolizes the disciples' willingness to share the Good News with others.

Preparation

Begin by preparing a treasure. An Easter basket filled with lots of candy works well. Make sure to include twice as much candy as the entire group will need. If your group meets at the same time as other groups, arrange with another leader or catechist to make a quick visit to their room to share the candy. If no other group is available, have the youth share treasure candy with their family or friends after the period. The impact is better, however, if they can share the candy immediately with other youth.

Next, the clues need to be prepared. Write each of the following clues and note on a separate piece of paper:

1. Your treasure is inside.
2. Your treasure is near a crucifix.
3. Your treasure is in a place we gather to pray.
4. Your treasure is near the Bible.
5. Your treasure is near an altar.
6. Your treasure is between the altar, the Bible, and the crucifix.
7. When you find your treasure there will be instructions.
8. You must follow the treasure instructions.

9. You now have enough clues for your search. Good luck.

10. "Why do you seek the living one among the dead?" Your treasure has been with you and remains closer to you than you think. Where else do you gather each week to learn about Jesus?

11. Note: Congratulations, you have found your treasure. Before you eat this candy, go and share some first with others.

The note should be clearly visible in or on the treasure basket. The basket's location is top secret and must be kept from the youth until the very end. Make arrangements with someone to have it placed in your meeting room after everyone has left to earn the clues. Ask him or her to place it between the table, the Bible, and the crucifix.

Remember, these clues are written with the assumption that your group normally meets in a room with a Bible, a table, and a crucifix. If your meeting room or gathering area does not have these items, bring them for this period and arrange them separately in your space.

Clue number 10 along with the ace bandage and cloths (see supply list following this section) should be placed near the altar, crucifix, and lector stand in church. If the church is not available during this period, try a side chapel. The youth may need a subtle hint during their search that the side chapel contains most of these items.

Next, find a site, preferably outside, where the youth can run a relay race. Mark with masking tape the start and midlines about twenty to thirty yards apart. While you are looking for a site, pick a place suitable for modified hide-and-seek.

At this point you are ready to introduce the activity. Begin by asking the group to name the things that happened on Easter morning according to the Gospel. Write their answers on the board. Direct the discussion such that the list includes the following: Jesus rose from the grave; Mary of Magdala discovered an empty tomb; the disciples raced to the tomb; the disciples found the burial cloths and head cloth; Mary of Magdala and the disciples were confused; one disciple saw and believed.

Use their list to summarize the Gospel events: there was a race, they were looking for Jesus, and everyone was trying to make sense of what happened. Announce that since this happened on Easter morning, the group will repeat similar events today. Explain the point of this activity is to find the hidden treasure. If they find it and follow the directions contained within before the end of the period, they will get to share in the candy.

Explain that the group must work together to earn the nine clues needed to lead them to the treasure. Clues are earned by racing and searching within the allotted time. The clues will be awarded after all nine have been earned. Only by combining all nine clues will the group be able to find the treasure.

Announce they have already earned the first clue by explaining the Gospel events of the first Easter morning. The rest will require more effort. Take the group out to the relay race site and show the start and midlines. Multiply the number of youth by ten seconds and announce they must run the course in relay style within that time in order to earn clue two. Ask the youth to form one line behind the starting line. Explain they must run to the midline and return to tag the next runner. Announce aloud the elapsed time during the race in order to add drama to their efforts. Note the team's time for the race and announce if they earned clue two. Have the group run it again using their first time as the standard to beat. Keep racing until they have earned the clues two through five. If the group is having difficulty meeting the time, set another obtainable time.

The remaining clues will be earned by playing a modified version of hide-and-seek. Take the youth to the hide-and-seek site and explain their next challenge is to work together to find the item (resurrection crucifix, lectionary, or Bible) within the allotted time. Ask the youth to close their eyes at a place designated as base. While the youth are closing their eyes, hide the item somewhere in the designated area. Return to base, invite them to open their eyes, and explain they have two minutes to find the item. Again, keep time aloud to add drama to the search. If the group is successful, announce they are awarded another clue. Continue playing rounds until all nine of the clues are earned. Feel free to vary the allotted time or be creative hiding the item.

At this point, explain they need to combine their clues in order to find the treasure. Emphasize teamwork. Distribute the nine clues dividing them among different youth, and ask each youth to read their clue aloud. If the main church is occupied and a side chapel is required for clue 10, make certain to give subtle hints in order to direct their search accordingly.

With luck, the youth will realize there is no treasure to be found in church and will discover clue 10. Be prepared to direct them to the clue if they do not find it on their own. They might need help figuring out the meeting room is the treasure site. It is a good idea to be prepared to help fill in any gaps if their search takes too long. When the treasure is found, make sure they read and follow the directions. Have the youth share the candy with the other group or with their family and friends as described above. After sharing the candy, take the youth to the reflection area.

Supply List

- ☐ Easter basket filled with candy
- ☐ ten clues and a note
- ☐ watch with a second hand
- ☐ an ace bandage rolled up and cloths
- ☐ masking tape
- ☐ crucifix, Bible, and table for the meeting room (many rooms already furnish this)
- ☐ resurrection crucifix, lectionary, or Bible for hiding

Reflection

Read aloud John 20:1–9.

Questions for Discussion

- ☐ What did the activity have to do with the Gospel?
- ☐ What did Mary think when she found the tomb empty?
- ☐ How was your response to figuring out the nine clues similar to the disciples' response that Jesus had been removed from the tomb?
- ☐ In the activity, how did you feel when you went into the church and did not find the treasure?
- ☐ How do you suppose Mary and the disciples felt when they found the empty tomb?
- ☐ How do you react when you hear amazing or unexpected news?
- ☐ What happened to the beloved disciple when he went into the tomb and saw the burial clothes and the rolled-up head cloth instead of Jesus?
- ☐ How do you use your eyesight to experience God?
- ☐ What are some ways you determine if what you hear is true or not?
- ☐ How did Jesus' resurrection change things for the disciples and others?
- ☐ How does Jesus' resurrection help us face difficult times in our life?
- ☐ How do you know in your heart that Jesus' message of love is true?
- ☐ What signs of Jesus' resurrection have you discovered in your life?
- ☐ When you finally found the candy in the activity, what did the note tell you to do?
- ☐ What have you discovered from this Gospel and how can you apply it in your life?
- ☐ In the next few days, how can you share God's love with others through your actions and attitudes?

Catechumenate Connection

Guide the neophytes to reflect upon how their entering the church is a new beginning to their life. Allow them to talk about how they felt entering the community. How does this experience parallel the experience of Mary and the disciples when they realized Jesus had risen?

Invite the inquirers, catechumens, and candidates to read section 640 in the *Catechism of the Catholic Church*. How do they feel about this resurrection story? What message do they find for their lives right now? What would they like to explore more about Jesus' life? What questions do they have about the Catholic faith? Invite the youth as a group to compile a list of these questions. Perhaps the group can research some of these questions each week during a portion of the meeting time.

2nd Sunday of Easter (ABC)

Readings

A	B	C
Acts 2:42–47	Acts 4:32–35	Acts 5:12–16
Psalm 118:2–4, 13–15, 22–24	Psalm 118:2–4, 13–15, 22–24	Psalm 118:2–4, 13–15, 22–24
1 Peter 1:3–9	1 John 5:1–6	Revelation 1:9–11a, 12–13, 17–19
John 20:19–31	John 20:19–31	John 20:19–31

Theme

Read John 20:19–31. "Unless I see the mark of the nails in his hands and put my finger into the nailmarks and put my hand into his side, I will not believe." With these words, Thomas, in this week's Gospel, conveys the heart of his faith struggle. For Thomas, hearsay was not enough. He trusted only his senses. If he could touch and see Jesus, then, and only then, would he believe.

Interestingly, Jesus does not judge or condemn Thomas for his faith struggle. Instead, Jesus extends his body to Thomas in order to strengthen his faith. For it is faith and trust which Jesus wants for Thomas, even if it must come through the physical senses. Thomas responds to Jesus with perhaps the most faithful proclamation found in all the Gospels, "My Lord and my God!" Just as Thomas struggled with doubt and came to believe in Jesus' resurrection through sight and touch, we, too, are called to deepen our faith by finding God in the ordinary experiences, people, and circumstances of our life.

Looking closely at the text, the passage begins with the disciples behind locked doors in fear of the Jews. Invite the youth to explore why the disciples must have been so fearful. As Jesus appeared, he immediately wished them peace, showed his hands, and gave them the gift of the Holy Spirit. Help the youth discover how these amazing incidents must have affected the disciples. How would they have felt if they were there? What do they suppose it meant to be given the Holy Spirit and the ability to forgive or retain sins?

Later, when Thomas heard of this, he was not convinced. Let the youth explain what they think Thomas must have thought of this wild story. How do they tell if something is true or not? What questions do they have about faith? Thomas trusted his senses, what do the youth trust to reveal the truth?

A week later Thomas was present when Jesus appeared. How do the youth imagine Thomas felt at this point? Instead of criticizing Thomas, Jesus offered proof. Encourage the youth to challenge and explore their faith. What do they really believe? Where do they find signs of God's love? Jesus says those who believe without seeing are blessed. How would the youth explain what Jesus means by this?

Activity Summary

The activity is designed to let the youth use touch to discern whether they are being told the truth. In doing so, they will come to better understand Thomas' faith struggle. The object is to let the youth use this experience to reflect upon how they touch and see God's presence in their own lives.

The activity consists of ten rounds that begin with the leader announcing the identity of an object inside a paper bag. The youth are invited to record on paper whether the leader's description is accurate or not. They will then be given an opportunity to reach into the bag and feel the object. Returning to their paper, they are again invited to record if the announcement was accurate or not. They will also get to write a description of the object based on what they felt. The youth with the most detailed and accurate description is recognized. Play continues through ten rounds with ten different objects.

Bridging the Activity and Reading

☐ In the activity, what the leader sometimes says is in the bag is unbelievable. This is similar to what Thomas heard from the other disciples about Jesus. It was unbelievable to Thomas.

☐ Touching the object to help discern if the leader is telling the truth represents Thomas' need to touch Jesus in order to believe what the disciples told him.

☐ Revealing the object in the activity represents Jesus revealing himself to Thomas and the others.

Preparation

Prepare for the activity by gathering ten grocery bags and ten easily identifiable small household objects that are safe to handle. Examples might include a baseball, a pencil sharpener, a stuffed animal, or a roll of masking tape. Try to find at least one object that will sound unbelievable when announced, such as a small glass elephant. When announcing the item in this bag, simply state that there is an elephant in the bag. Next, place one object inside each bag and staple across the top. Leave a five-inch opening at the top to allow space to put a hand inside without seeing into the bag.

Begin by distributing paper and pencils to each youth. Explain that ten items have been carefully concealed inside grocery bags. These ten bags represent ten rounds of play. Starting with the first bag, the leader will announce what is inside. The leader may be telling the truth or playing a trick. Each player will record whether or not he or she believes the leader by writing *true* or *false* on his or her paper.

Next, each player will come forward and be given a few seconds to reach inside the bag and feel the object. Returning to his or her seat, each player will again write whether or not they believe the leader. This should reveal the accuracy of their first guess. Next, each player will write a detailed description of what was felt in the bag. Players are encouraged to envision the object and use their imagination to describe characteristics such as color, size, and weight. When finished, the players will read their descriptions aloud. The bag is then opened and the object revealed. Congratulate the player with the most accurate and detailed description according to the leader's judgment. Each of the rounds is played in this same manner.

For the best effect, use false descriptions in about half the rounds mixing the sequence to avoid any recognizable pattern. Announce these bogus identities in your best poker face and ask the youth to write *true* or *false*. Also, encourage the youth to watch the facial expressions of those touching the object. The expressions on their face may reveal the accuracy of their guess. Hold the bag while players walk by and place their hand inside. Make sure no one peaks into the bag. Allow each player enough time to determine the object's identity, however, no one should be given more than fifteen seconds. When finished, move to the reflection area.

Supply List

- ☐ ten paper grocery bags
- ☐ ten common household items
- ☐ stapler
- ☐ pencil and paper for each youth

Reflection

Read aloud John 20:19–31.

Questions for Discussion

- ☐ What did the activity have to do with the Gospel?
- ☐ Why do you think Thomas needed proof to believe Jesus was alive?
- ☐ What sort of unbelievable things have others told you that you needed proof to believe?
- ☐ How do you know when to believe something and when not to believe it?
- ☐ How do you know what to believe about God and what not to believe?
- ☐ What was it like to feel the object and know without a doubt what it was?
- ☐ How did your expression change when you identified the object?
- ☐ Although you could not see or prove what you felt in the grocery bag, many times you knew what it was. How is this like our faith?
- ☐ How do our lives change when we become close to God?
- ☐ What would you say if someone asked you to prove that God exists?
- ☐ Why is it important for each of us to have our own experiences of God rather than to only rely upon other's experiences?
- ☐ Other than praying and going to Mass, what are some ways you see and touch God's presence in your life?
- ☐ Why were the disciples so afraid when they were locked in the room?

☐ How do you suppose they felt when Jesus appeared, offered them peace, and gave them the Holy Spirit?

☐ What did it mean to be given the Holy Spirit and the ability to forgive or retain sins?

☐ Jesus says, "Blessed are those who have not seen and have believed." What do you think this means?

☐ What have you discovered from this Gospel and how can you apply it in your life?

☐ In the next few days, what can you do to reveal God's presence to someone who doubts?

Catechumenate Connection

This Sunday's Gospel give us the opportunity to reflect on why we believe in God. Discuss with the inquirers, catechumens, candidates, and neophytes why they believe God exists. As they explore their spirituality, how do they find God being revealed in their lives? Why have they joined or why are they considering joining the Catholic Church?

Catholic means universal (*Catechism of the Catholic Church* §830, §831), which reminds us that Jesus meant the Good News to be shared with all people. Discuss how the community of believers shares their faith with one another. How is our faith shared with our society? Catholics look to experience God not only in the sacraments and Scriptures but in the presence of all people as well. Reaching out to others is also a way to touch and find God. How do charitable works show that our faith is real? What service projects does our parish support? With which of these projects could the group become involved? What other types of parish ministries are available to the group?

We believe that faith is a gift of the Spirit (*Catechism of the Catholic Church* §153). What do they do with this gift? How can they increase their faith? How can people refuse the gift of faith? When it comes to faith, is it true that you must use it or lose it? Explain.

Explore how others reveal to us that God is alive in their hearts. How are these people an example to them? In their daily lives how can they show to others that their faith is real?

3rd Sunday of Easter (A)

✝ *Faith* ✝

Readings

Acts 2:14, 22–33
Psalm 16:1–2, 5, 7–8, 9–10, 11
1 Peter 1:17–21
Luke 24:13–35

Theme

Read Luke 24:13–35. The story of the two disciples' trip to Emmaus is a wonderful account of how Jesus is revealed through Scriptures and the breaking of bread to those taking a faith journey. The disciples struggled with all they had witnessed about Jesus: his mighty deeds and words, his crucifixion and death, their dashed hopes of Jesus as Israel's redeemer, and now wild reports of angels announcing his resurrection. What were the disciples to make of all of this? They had many experiences to sort out. What was needed was a context, a new perspective through which to interpret these events and make sense of them.

At this point the story takes on highly liturgical connotations as the unrecognized Jesus provides the needed scriptural and historical context for these events. Interestingly, it was the broadening experience of listening to the Scriptures along with the experience of breaking bread that revealed Jesus' presence and empowered the disciples to understand and believe in the resurrection. We, too, are called to a broader experience of Christ through Scriptures and breaking bread that we might deepen our faith and share it with others as the two disciples did upon their return from Emmaus.

Looking closely at the Gospel, the disciples were downcast when questioned by the stranger. Invite the youth to describe how the disciples must have felt. How do they think faith and hope are related? What sort of things challenges their faith?

As the disciples were struggling to make sense of all that had happened, they needed a new perspective, one that could take their focus from recent events and put it into scriptural context. How do the youth feel Jesus helped them with this? Why do they suppose it was important for the disciples to understand the scriptural context relating to Jesus' life and death? How do the Scriptures help them grow closer to God?

As the three of them shared the bread, the disciples recognized the stranger as Jesus. He vanished from their midst and they were filled with joy returning immediately to Jerusalem to share their faith experience. Invite the youth to discuss what this means. How did the disciples' feelings change from the beginning of this story? Lead the youth to discover the death and resurrection cycle in this reading. Why do they suppose this cycle is repeated in so many Gospel stories? What does this cycle say about how we live our faith?

Activity Summary

This activity is designed to simulate the struggle faced by the disciples while on the road to Emmaus. The disciples tried to make sense of the recent events they had just witnessed, but were hopeless without the historical and scriptural context that Jesus later provided. Likewise, the youth will attempt to determine the significance of various items in a paper bag, without the needed context. Later, with the leader's assistance, they will realize that collectively they have the ingredients of a cookie. The intent is to help them discover their need for broader perspectives, especially how Scripture, Eucharist, and community reveal God's broader perspective.

The activity begins by challenging the youth to solve the mystery of the paper bag. They are asked to identify the contents of their bag and the significance of the items inside. Each youth is given a paper bag containing three items. One of the items is a cookie ingredient such as flour or sugar, while the other items serve as decoys, completely unrelated to the cookie. The idea is to have each youth assume he or she is trying to figure out the contents of his or her individual bag. Each round they explore the contents with one of their five senses and record what the items are and their significance. After the last round, they will realize the real significance of their item: Their ingredient is one of many that form a cookie. With careful execution and attention to detail, this realization will occur as the youth begin sharing a large cookie together. The intent is to have their realization parallel the disciples' recognition of Jesus during the breaking of bread.

Bridging the Activity and Reading

- ☐ Struggling to understand the significance of the items in the individual bags represents the disciples struggle to make sense of the events of Jesus' life, death, and resurrection.
- ☐ The leader helping the youth focus on the bigger picture (all items in all the bags) symbolizes the stranger, Jesus, helping the disciples understand how Jesus' death and resurrection fit into the context of Scriptures.
- ☐ Sharing the cookie together represents Jesus breaking bread with the disciples.
- ☐ Recognizing the contents of the plastic bag as ingredients to a cookie symbolizes the disciples' recognition of Jesus through the breaking of bread.

Preparation

Bake a cookie in a pizza-type pan large enough to be broken into pieces and shared among all the youth. The ingredients should not be easily recognizable by the youth. For example, a snickerdoodle or sugar cookie works better than a chocolate chip cookie.

Next, prepare a paper bag for each youth. Begin by placing a small amount of one of the cookie ingredients into an individual plastic bag and sealing it. Do the same for each of the cookie's ingredients and place each of these plastic bags into an individual paper lunch bag. Only one ingredient is needed per bag. However, if possible try to include a sample of each ingredient somewhere so the entire cookie's ingredients are represented. If the group is large, consider duplicating some of the more difficult-to-recognize ingredients, such as baking soda or cream of tarter. When finished, place two small, unrelated objects into each paper bag. Include different items in each bag. Consider using items without sharp edges or points such as small balls, paper wads, or spoons. Staple shut each lunch bag. You should now have two small objects and a plastic bag containing one ingredient stapled inside a paper lunch bag for each youth.

When introducing the activity to the youth, choose your words very carefully, so no hints are given. In order for the activity to work, the youth must infer from your words that they are to identify only the contents of their own bag. Avoid using the word *ingredient* in the instructions. One suggestion is to announce the object of the activity is to solve the mystery of the paper bag. Each player will receive a paper bag containing a few items along with paper and a pencil. Five rounds will be played. Each round begins with the opportunity to use one of their five senses to learn about the items. After a brief inspection, each player will write down the objects' identity and significance. Significance in this setting refers to any special meaning they might discover in their bags. Encourage the youth to pay careful attention to all the clues given by their senses when recording their thoughts after each round.

Distribute paper and pencils to the youth and ask them to number their paper one through five leaving spaces for several lines between each number. Next, place a bag in front of each youth with strict orders not to touch it until instructed. Once all bags are distributed, ask them to carefully pick up their bag by the top, and gently shake it. Invite the youth to consider its weight and how it sounds when shaken. When finished, ask them to put their bags down, and write all that their senses tell them about the objects next to the number one on their paper. Ask them to also record a guess about the items and their significance.

After all guesses are recorded, ask them to carefully open the top of their bag without looking inside. It may be a good idea to have the youth close their eyes for this round. Explain that one of the objects in the bag is inside a plastic bag. Invite the youth to place their hand in the paper bag and touch the objects. The item in the plastic bag must be touched through the plastic bag. When finished, ask the youth to remove their hand from the bag and record everything their senses tell them about the objects along with a guess about their identities and significance beside the number two on their sheet.

Next, ask the youth to remove all the contents of their paper bag and place them on the table in front of them. Invite the youth to carefully observe the contents using only sight. They should not touch, smell, or use any other senses for this round. Encourage the youth to observe the color, size, texture, and anything else interesting. Ask them to record these observations along with a guess about the object's identities and significance next to the number three on their sheets.

Explain that round four will focus on the sense of smell. Ask the youth to carefully open their plastic bag and smell its contents. Also, invite them to smell their other objects. Have them focus on any familiar odors or anything that might give them clues they have missed. When finished, instruct them to again record their findings, guess, and significance on their sheet beside the number four.

Round five deals with the sense of taste. Invite them to taste the contents of the plastic bag by placing a small amount on their tongue and savoring the flavor for a moment. Strongly discourage any tasting of the other objects. When finished, invite each youth to record their findings, guess, and significance next to the number five.

Ask if anyone's first guess was the same as his or her last guess. Next, ask each youth to read the clues and guesses he or she wrote starting with number one and ending with number five. After each youth answers, move on to the next youth without revealing if the guess is correct.

When finished, remind them how in the beginning they were asked to identify their objects and state their significance. Ask for a show of hands from those who felt this was a difficult challenge. Invite them to consider that they may have been too focused on the small picture. Invite them to focus not so much upon what they have in front of them, but to look at the bigger picture. At this point, bring out the cookie, break it apart, and share it with each youth. Ask the youth to think as a group of what they have in their bags; emphasize the plural here. If they still have not figured out that they each have ingredients for a cookie, explain that the significance can be found in what they are eating. Continue to give them hints until they answer correctly.

Supply List

- [ ] one large cookie
- [ ] small amounts of the cookie's ingredients placed into plastic bags
- [ ] enough brown lunch bags for each youth to have one bag
- [ ] two different, small objects to place in each brown bag (examples include small balls, erasers, or paper clips)
- [ ] pencils
- [ ] paper

Reflection

Read aloud Luke 24:13–35.

Questions for Discussion

- [ ] What did the activity have to do with the Gospel?
- [ ] In the activity, what were you trying to understand?
- [ ] How do you suppose the disciples felt as they began their journey to Emmaus?
- [ ] What were the disciples trying to understand?
- [ ] What questions about God do people your age try to understand?

- ☐ In the activity, why was it necessary to look at the contents of all the bags?
- ☐ How did the leader help you to look at the bigger picture?
- ☐ How did the stranger help the disciples look at the bigger picture?
- ☐ What are some examples of how people have helped you understand things better by getting you to focus on the bigger picture?
- ☐ What are some ways God's perspectives differ from how people see things?
- ☐ How does reading Scripture and learning about Jesus help us become closer to God?
- ☐ In the activity, how did sharing the cookie help you recognize the significance of the ingredient in your bag?
- ☐ How did the disciples feel once they recognized Jesus while sharing bread?
- ☐ How did this experience change them from when they began their journey?
- ☐ What are some ways people change when they experience God closely?
- ☐ How does the church use Scriptures and the breaking of bread to experience God?
- ☐ Who are people through whom you have experienced God's presence?
- ☐ What did the disciples immediately do once they recognized Jesus?
- ☐ In the activity, how did the other items in the bag interfere with your focus on the significance of the cookie ingredient?
- ☐ What are things in our life that take our focus away from God?
- ☐ What have you discovered from this Gospel and how can you apply it in your life?
- ☐ In the next few days, what are some ways you can share your faith with others?

Catechumenate Connection

This Gospel gives ample opportunity to discuss the four ways the church experiences God through liturgy. Explore with the inquirers, catechumens, candidates, and neophytes how Catholics experience God through the word, the Eucharist, the priest, and others. Begin by reviewing the word *liturgy*. Invite them to read section 1069 from the *Catechism of the Catholic Church* and discuss the definition.

Invite the youth to reflect on the Gospel. How was Christ revealed to the disciples through the Scriptures? How can Christ's presence be experienced during the readings at Mass? Invite the youth to describe the attitude and attentiveness of a person during Mass who believes he or she will experience God in the readings. How do they use Scripture to help them on their spiritual journey?

Next invite the youth to explore how God is present through the Eucharist. In the Gospel, when did the disciples recognize Jesus? Explain how the church remembers Jesus during the Eucharistic celebration. What meaning do they find in sharing a meal with their family or friends?

Finally, emphasize that we recognize God in each other. How did the disciples' openness to the stranger change them from being downcast, sad, and confused to energetic, faith-filled disciples? How can our openness to others transform us? How do we recognize Jesus in others? How do others recognize Jesus in us?

3rd Sunday of Easter (B)

✝   *Faith*   ✝

Readings

Acts 3:13–15, 17–19
Psalm 4:2, 4, 7–8, 9
1 John 2:1–5a
Luke 24:35–48

Theme

Read Luke 24:35–48. The Gospel passage this Third Sunday of Easter is a continuation of the Emmaus story. As the two disciples are telling the others about their amazing experience at Emmaus, behold, Jesus makes another appearance. This time he appears to all the disciples and others who were gathered. Clearly Jesus wanted to comfort those he loved and build their faith. All the amazing stories of Jesus' resurrection, his many wonderful deeds, his life and teachings based upon love and forgiveness, all of these things were swimming in their heads. But, to really experience and witness in the flesh one who had resurrected, never to die again, this was something that would validate everything. To experience the resurrected Jesus would seal their faith and make sense of all they had witnessed.

And so it was that Jesus appeared to the group and showed his wounds. He ate with them and comforted them. He replaced their terror with peace, amazement, and a wonderful joy. Naturally, Jesus took this opportunity to open their minds to the Scriptures, to all that was written about him in the law of Moses, by the prophets, and in the Psalms. In revealing himself in this way, those gathered would be able to begin putting all the pieces of their faith together. This Third Sunday of Easter we, too, are called to put together the pieces of our faith. Where do we find God revealed in our lives? How do we struggle to become more forgiving, more loving, and more compassionate? How do our actions and words reveal God's presence to others?

In exploring the text, consider explaining the context of this passage. Invite the youth to discuss how those gathered must have felt listening to the disciples before Jesus appeared. How did they feel once Jesus appeared? Discuss with the youth why they think Jesus appeared to the group. What was Jesus trying to accomplish?

Jesus showed them the wounds in his hands and feet, he invited them to touch him, and he ate in front of them. Ask the youth why they think Jesus did this? How did those gathered change after Jesus did these things? How do they suppose seeing Jesus resurrected from the dead changed their understanding of Jesus? Invite the youth to share examples from their lives of how a person's actions have changed what they thought of that person. What do people's actions reveal about them? What are some ways the youth have experienced God's love through the actions of others?

Jesus reminded them of the words he spoke while he was with them and he opened their minds to understand how the Scriptures referred to him. Invite the youth to discuss why Jesus did this. How do they suppose this helped the faith of those gathered? How do Scriptures help them build their faith?

Activity Summary

In the Gospel, Jesus builds up the faith of those he loves by revealing himself through his actions and words. This activity is designed to parallel these events with a version of the game, charades. The youth will be divided into teams and take turns guessing the name of a mystery person. A youth will be selected from the guessing team to be the clue giver. This clue giver will have a total of sixty seconds to provide clues to his or her teammates. The first thirty seconds he or she will be required to act in ways that would reveal the mystery person's identity. If a teammate shouts the correct identity in this period the team receives two points. The second thirty seconds of the round will allow the clue giver to use words to reveal the mystery person's identity. A correct guess in this second period is awarded with one point to the team.

The idea is to let the youth appreciate how our actions and words reveal something of ourselves. Discovering the mystery person's identity through the actions and words of a teammate will provide the youth insights into how Jesus nurtured the faith of those he loved with his words and actions. As Jesus revealed his divine identity in this way, so, too, will the youth discover how they can reveal the God dwelling within themselves to others.

Bridging the Activity and Reading

- ☐ The clue giver's use of actions to reveal the mystery person's identity represents Jesus' use of actions (appearing, showing his wounds, and eating) to reveal his identity.
- ☐ The clue giver speaking to reveal the mystery person's identity symbolizes Jesus speaking about how Scriptures revealed his own identity.
- ☐ Guessing the mystery person's identity based on the clues represents how those gathered came to know Jesus' real identity.

Preparation

Preparation is easy. Before for the session, write the names of people on note cards. Make sure to choose people who are easily recognizable to the youth. The people could include actors, actresses, singers, political figures, and even local celebrities. You might also consider choosing people from your parish, such as the DRE, priest, or deacon. The number of names needed will be determined by the amount of time you have for this activity. To ensure there are enough names, plan on one name for every ninety seconds of activity time. Fold the note cards and place them in a basket, hat, or other container.

When announcing the activity to the youth, explain that they will be playing a type of charades. The group will be divided into teams. The team with the most points at the end wins. For each round, a team will choose a clue giver. The clue giver will pick a note card and silently read the name on the card. The object of the round is for the clue giver to get his or her teammates to guess the name on the note card. The clue giver will be given thirty seconds to act like the mystery person. For instance, if a famous basketball player is chosen, the clue giver might act like he or she is playing basketball. During these thirty seconds, the clue giver must only use actions and gestures to get his or her teammates to identify the mystery person. Talking or making any sounds by the clue giver is strictly prohibited during this thirty seconds. If any member of the team correctly shouts the name of the mystery person within the thirty seconds, the team will receive two points.

If the team does not guess the mystery person in the first thirty seconds, they will be given a second thirty seconds to earn only one point. This time the clue giver will be allowed to speak. He or she must only say words and phrases that the mystery person would likely say. The clue giver will not be allowed to say the name of the person, describe the person, or give any other details or hints about the person. If this rule is violated in any way, the team will not be awarded any points for the round. The leader will act as referee and all decisions are final.

When all understand, divide the group into teams. Invite the first team to choose a clue giver. Next, invite the clue giver to select a note card. Give the clue giver a few seconds to think about the selected person. When the clue giver is ready, begin timing. If the team has not guessed the mystery person within thirty seconds, invite the clue giver to use words and phrases that the mystery person would likely say. Pay careful attention to make sure all the rules governing the second thirty seconds are followed. Award the team the correct amount of points and invite the next team to choose a clue giver. Be certain each team is given the same amount of rounds to score. Continue playing as long as time allows.

Supply List

- ☐ prepared note cards
- ☐ basket, hat, or other container for the note cards
- ☐ stopwatch or watch with a second hand
- ☐ paper and pencil or a chalkboard and chalk to keep score

Reflection

Read aloud Luke 24:35–48.

Questions for Discussion

☐ What did the activity have to do with the Gospel?

☐ How do you suppose the disciples and the others who were there felt listening to the story about Jesus before he appeared?

☐ How do you suppose they felt as soon as Jesus appeared?

☐ Why do you think Jesus appeared to this group; what was he trying to accomplish?

☐ In the activity, what kinds of things did people do in the first thirty seconds to give clues?

☐ Why did Jesus invite them to touch him, show them his hands and feet, and eat in front of them?

☐ How do you suppose those gathered changed after Jesus did these things?

☐ In the activity, how did you feel the moment you identified the mystery person?

☐ How do you suppose those who saw Jesus resurrected from the dead that day changed their understanding of him?

☐ What are some examples in your life of how someone did something that made you change what you thought of that person?

☐ What do people's actions reveal about them?

☐ What are some ways you have experienced God's love through the actions of others?

☐ What are some ways people have spoken to you that helped you experience love, forgiveness, or patience?

☐ In the activity, how did using words in the second thirty seconds make it easier to identify the mystery person?

☐ After showing the people he was really alive and resurrected, Jesus spoke to them of how the Scriptures and prophets had written about him. Why do you suppose Jesus did this?

☐ How do you think this helped build the faith of those gathered?

☐ How do Scriptures and the words of others help you build your faith?

☐ What have you discovered from this Gospel and how can you apply it in your life?

☐ In the next few days, what can you do to show others that God is dwelling within you?

Catechumenate Connection

This Gospel gives ample opportunity to discuss the four ways the church experiences God through liturgy. Explore with the inquirers, catechumens, candidates, and neophytes how Catholics experience God through the word, the Eucharist, the priest, and the people gathered. Begin by reviewing the word *liturgy*. Invite them to read section 1069 from the *Catechism of the Catholic Church* and discuss the definition.

Invite the youth to reflect on the Gospel. How was Christ revealed to the disciples through the Scriptures? How can Christ's presence be experienced during the readings at Mass? Invite the youth to describe the attitude and attentiveness of a person during Mass who believes he or she will experience God in the readings. How do they use Scripture to help them on their spiritual journey?

Next invite the youth to explore how God is present through the Eucharist. In the Gospel, when did the disciples recognize Jesus? Explain how the Church remembers Jesus during the Eucharistic celebration. What meaning do they find in sharing a meal with their family or friends?

Finally, emphasize that we recognize God in each other. How did the disciples' openness to Jesus change them from being afraid and confused to joyful, amazed, and faith-filled disciples? How can our openness to others transform us? How do we recognize Jesus in others? How do others recognize Jesus in us?

3rd Sunday of Easter (C)

Recognizing God   ✝   *Discipleship*

Readings

Acts 5:27–32, 40b–41
Psalm 30:2, 4, 5–6, 11–12, 13
Revelation 5:11–14
John 21:1–19

Theme

Read John 21:1–19. John's Gospel this week has two main ideas woven into this highly symbolic account of Jesus' appearance. First, the disciples recognize God's presence in the stranger through the miracle of the filled fishing nets. Recognizing Jesus changed the disciples' long empty night of fishing into a joyous breakfast feast. Likewise, for us, too, it is the recognition of God in our lives that promises to change our emptiness to joy.

The second theme is a call to discipleship. Jesus asks Peter three times if he loves him. Each time Jesus tells Peter to feed or tend his sheep. The pastoral language of feeding sheep is Peter's call to continue the ministry of Jesus, a call that we as followers of Christ share. Confessing one's love is important, but acting upon that love brings about a new reality.

In reviewing the Gospel, invite the youth to discuss how the disciples must have felt after a night of unsuccessful fishing. How do they think this changed with the miraculous catch? How did Jesus' appearance change the disciples? Why did Simon Peter take a flying leap into the sea?

This is a wonderful opportunity for the youth to reflect on how they recognize God's presence in others. With whom do they experience patience, forgiveness, kindness, or compassion? How do they recognize God in themselves? When do they feel particularly close to God? How is God present in their thoughts, feelings, and desires? Let them explore how recognizing God in their life helps them love others more.

After breakfast Jesus and Peter had a little heart-to-heart discussion. Why do the youth think Jesus asked Peter three times if he loved him? Why did Jesus tell Peter, "Feed my sheep" and "Tend my sheep?" What connection do the youth see between real love and actions? How do they show their love through actions?

The final part of the reading talks about Peter's death. How do the youth feel about the risks of loving unconditionally? What are some of the risks they see in loving others unconditionally? What risks are they willing to take in order to live God's law of love?

Activity Summary

Two different activities are designed to capture the two themes emerging from the Gospel this week. First, we are called to recognize the presence of God just as the disciples recognized Jesus through the miraculous catch of fish. Recognizing God is a search that leads us to others and to an acceptance of ourselves. The first activity will allow the youth to list the good qualities they recognize in each other. These lists will then be read to give each youth an opportunity to recognize which qualities their peers see in them. The goal is to let the youth recognize God's presence in themselves and in others.

The second theme is a call to put this recognition of God into action as followers of Christ. Just as Jesus instructed Peter to feed his sheep, we, too, are called to share our faith and reach out to others. The second activity is preparing for and throwing a party. The idea is to let the youth do something to reach out to others in a way that makes them feel welcomed. The intent is to help the youth reflect on ways they can share God's presence with others in their life.

Bridging the Activity and Readings

☐ Recognizing and writing the good qualities the youth see in others is symbolic of how the disciples recognized Jesus by the miracle he performed.

☐ Listening to the good qualities others wrote about them and the effect that experience had upon each youth represents how the disciples changed when Jesus became present to them.

☐ The instructions for preparing the party and providing food for the guests represents Jesus telling Peter to feed and tend his sheep.

☐ Sharing your good qualities with others in the party symbolizes the type of life awaiting Peter when Jesus asked him to follow him.

Preparation

Prepare for the first activity by numerically listing each youth's name on poster board, newsprint, or chalkboard. Make sure the names are written large enough for the entire group to read. For groups with more than twenty youth, consider dividing them into smaller groups. Have other youth leaders or catechists lead each group through the exercise simultaneously. A list will need to be prepared for each group. Gather paper and a pencil for each youth.

Preparation for the second activity is a bit more involved. Begin by making arrangements to invite people to a party. Give yourself plenty of time, perhaps a week before the period, to find people. Consider other religious education classes, youth groups, or RCIA groups meeting at the same time as your group. Explain to these leaders how you would like to have your youth invite their group to a party toward the latter part of the period. If other groups are not available, consider inviting the youth's parents, siblings, neighbors, or friends. Give these folks a specific time and place to gather about halfway through your period. Explain to the guests how long you expect the party to last and that it will be followed by a discussion period.

Next, consider how many people will be attending the party and gather the needed items from the supply list following this section. Write steps for preparing a party on individual pieces of paper. Make sure to prepare at least one step for each youth even if the steps have to be duplicated. The steps should include:

- ☐ Make a welcome poster.
- ☐ Make an invitation.
- ☐ Deliver the invitation.
- ☐ Sweep the room.
- ☐ Hang the decorations.
- ☐ Blow up balloons.
- ☐ Hang the balloons.
- ☐ Plan something fun to do.
- ☐ Choose the music.
- ☐ Arrange the tables.
- ☐ Arrange the chairs.
- ☐ Cut the cake.
- ☐ Arrange the snacks.
- ☐ Pour the drinks.
- ☐ Arrange the plates and napkins.

At this point, you are ready to introduce the first activity. Distribute paper and pencils to each youth and ask them to number their paper top to bottom to correlate with the names on the posted list. Ask them to write on their paper one quality they admire about each member of the group next to that person's number. Encourage them to write something that person does that shows their goodness. Explain the lists will be read aloud to the group. When completed, collect each paper and quickly check each comment, making sure all are acceptable. Invite the group to listen carefully as you read a description of someone. Choose a number at random, and read the description written about the selected youth from each paper. When finished, invite them to guess whose description was read. Continue until descriptions of all the youth have been read and identified.

Once the first activity is completed, announce that they will have an opportunity to share their good qualities with others by throwing a party. Announce who will be coming to the party and explain the idea is to make them feel as welcome as possible. Distribute an instruction slip to each youth and explain they will need to work together to prepare for the party. The project has been divided into tasks. The slip they have will tell them what to do. If the group has fewer than fifteen youth, explain that some people may receive more than one instruction. If the group is larger than fifteen, two or more youth may share the same instruction.

Finally, it is a good idea to consider your time restraints. Announce how much time is left to finish the preparations. Keep an eye on the clock, and continue to announce the time remaining to keep the youth on task. Preparations must be finished with ample time for the party and reflection. When the preparations are ready, have the invitations delivered to the prearranged guests. Enjoy the party, but watch the clock so you can move the youth to the reflection area at the appropriate time.

Supply List

First Activity
- [ ] poster board, newsprint, or chalkboard
- [ ] paper and pencils

Second Activity
- [ ] white slips of paper with individual instructions for a party
- [ ] several staplers
- [ ] broom and dustpan
- [ ] crepe paper
- [ ] balloons
- [ ] tape
- [ ] cake
- [ ] plates, forks, napkins, and cups
- [ ] punch, juice, or pop
- [ ] party snacks such as pretzels, potato chips, or popcorn
- [ ] markers to make the invitation and welcome sign
- [ ] paper to make the invitation
- [ ] poster board for the welcome sign
- [ ] tape player or CD player
- [ ] several different tapes or CDs with popular music

Reflection

Read aloud John 21:1–19.

Questions for Discussion

- [ ] What did the activity have to do with the Gospel?
- [ ] How do you suppose the disciples felt after a night of unsuccessful fishing?
- [ ] How did Jesus' appearance and the miraculous catch change the disciples?
- [ ] Why did Simon Peter take a flying leap into the sea?
- [ ] What are some ways you recognize God's presence in other people?
- [ ] With whom do you experience patience, forgiveness, kindness, or compassion?
- [ ] How would things be different if people spent more time recognizing the good in others?
- [ ] In the activity, how did it feel hearing the goodness others see in you?
- [ ] How do you recognize God inside yourself?
- [ ] How does recognizing God in your life help you love others?

- ☐ Why do you think Jesus asked Peter three times if he loved him?
- ☐ What did Jesus mean when he told Peter, "Feed my sheep" and "Tend my sheep?"
- ☐ What ways did you make others feel welcome at the party?
- ☐ How is this like tending and feeding sheep?
- ☐ What are some other ways you can help feed and tend Jesus' sheep?
- ☐ Jesus predicted Peter would die because he followed him. What are some of the risks you take as a follower of Christ?
- ☐ What have you discovered from this Gospel and how can you apply it in your life?
- ☐ In the next few days, how can you look for God's presence in the people you meet or share God's presence with others?

Catechumenate Connection

The Gospel this week is particularly well suited to bridge the neophytes, candidates, catechumens, and inquirers into a reflection upon their spiritual journey. Invite them to identify people in whom they have been able to recognize God's presence. How have these people influenced their desire to grow closer to God? How do the youth feel God's presence in their life? What are some ways they sense God working in their life? In the Gospel, when Peter said he loved Jesus, Jesus told Peter to feed or tend his sheep. How do the youth feel they are being called to express their love for God? What opportunities are available for the youth to become involved in parish ministries? How do the youth feel about the risks involved with following Christ?

Catholics believe that all members of the church have a special calling from God to share their faith (*Catechism of the Catholic Church* §873). While the church is made up of many diverse people with different gifts, all these people share the same mission of spreading God's love and building up the faith. Invite the youth to discuss various ways people share faith and spread love. How do various professions work to build up God's kingdom? What are some ways they have experienced the faith of others?

4th Sunday of Easter (ABC)

God's Love   ✝   Trust

Readings

A	B	C
Acts 2:14a, 36–41	Acts 4:8–12	Acts 13:14, 43–52
Psalm 23:1–3a, 3b–4, 5, 6	Psalm 118:1, 8–9, 21–23, 26, 28, 29	Psalm 100:1–2, 3, 5
1 Peter 2:20b–25	1 John 3:1–2	Revelation 7:9, 14b–17
John 10:1–10	John 10:11–18	John 10:27–30

Theme

Read John 10:1–10, John 10:11–18, or John 10:27–30. The Fourth Sunday of Easter is also known as Good Shepherd Sunday. Each of the three liturgical years uses the Gospel this Sunday to focus on a different portion of the good shepherd discourse from John's tenth chapter. Year A features Jesus as the gate through which the sheep find salvation and eternal life. In Year B, the symbolism centers on Jesus as the good shepherd who lays down his life for the sheep and brings them into one fold. Year C's image of Jesus the shepherd emphasizes his role as provider of eternal life and protection.

Throughout these readings several common themes and beautiful images emerge. First, the shepherd's love for his sheep is an image rich with compassion, protection, and eternal life. Second, in each reading the sheep image seems to speak of the neediness or broken nature of humanity, a people incomplete and searching for leadership. Third, each reading features the sheep hearing or recognizing the shepherd's voice. And finally, each Gospel passage clearly states that Jesus the shepherd knows his sheep. Because these readings share so much in common, a single activity and session has been developed for use with any of these Gospels.

While exploring the Gospel, invite the youth to consider the image of Jesus as shepherd or gate. What do they think Jesus was trying to communicate about himself by using this image? How do they feel about the idea of God as a shepherd? How do they imitate this shepherd's love?

In the same way, explore with the youth the image of sheep. What do they know about sheep? What do they suppose Jesus was trying to say about humanity by using this image? How does the relationship between shepherd and sheep describe the relationship between God and his people?

Jesus also talks about how the sheep hear and recognize the shepherd's voice. Let the youth contemplate what it means to recognize the shepherd's voice. How do they listen for

God's voice? How would they describe people who listen to God? What are some of the challenges they face as they try to listen to God's voice?

Each of these readings also speaks of how the shepherd knows his sheep. Invite the youth to share how they feel about a God who knows them personally. How do they feel knowing that God knows them so well yet still loves them unconditionally?

Activity Summary

The activity for this Fourth Sunday of Easter is designed to capture the experience of the shepherd's love. The youth will be able to experience gentle guidance in their time of need followed by an opportunity to provide another with this same guidance. They will experience the neediness implied in the sheep image and discover the significance of recognizing the shepherd's voice. The goal is to help the youth discover how God loves them and how trusting God is a natural response to this love.

The activity begins with the youth divided into pairs. One of the pair is blindfolded while the sighted partner stands at a distance. Simultaneously each of the sighted youth calls their blindfolded partner's name. The blindfolded youth must find his or her partner by recognizing and moving toward the correct voice. Once the pair is united, they work as a team with the blindfolded youth following his or her partner's voice through a maze. When finished, they switch roles and repeat the activity.

Bridging the Activity and Reading

- ☐ The sighted partner represents Jesus as the shepherd in the Gospel.
- ☐ The blindfolded partner represents the sheep.
- ☐ Listening for the partner's voice in the first part of the activity signifies the sheep recognizing the shepherd's voice.
- ☐ Leading the blindfolded partner safely through the maze to the candy at the end represents Jesus leading his sheep to eternal life.

Preparation

Begin by selecting a spacious site such as an outdoor area, gymnasium, or large meeting room. If the site is outside, make sure the area is level and free of holes and rocks. Using masking tape, create a maze on the floor or ground by placing the tape in parallel lines approximately two feet apart. Be creative by including many turns and twists to make the path feel like a maze. The idea is to make a meandering course, impossible for a blindfolded youth to walk without instruction. Be sure to make the path at least twenty yards in length. The final preparation is to gather blindfolds for half the youth and candy to award all the youth.

With these preparations in place, you are now ready to begin. If possible gather the youth a short distance from the maze for the first part of the activity. This will extend the experience in the second phase of the activity, as the blindfolded youth will be required to follow his or her sighted partner to the maze sight.

Begin by dividing the youth into pairs. If there are an odd number of youth, ask an aide or co-catechist to join in to complete another pair. Introduce the activity by announcing that they are about to undergo a two-part test of their listening, instructing, and teamwork skills. Throughout both parts of the activity, one member of the pair will be blindfolded. In the first part, each of the blindfolded youth will stand together in one section while their sighted partners are quietly moved to another place in the area. Then, simultaneously each of the sighted partners will begin calling their blindfolded partner's name. Those who are blindfolded must find their partner by recognizing and moving toward the correct voice. Once each pair is united, this first part is complete.

The activity's second part begins with the sighted partner leading the blindfolded partner to the maze site. Here the pair's ability to work together, give instruction, and listen closely will be challenged. Each of the blindfolded youth must walk through the maze without stepping outside its boundaries, guided only by the voice commands of his or her sighted partner. The partner cannot touch his or her blindfolded partner in anyway. If the blindfolded partner should step outside the tape boundary, he or she must take a giant step backward on the path. When the blindfolded youth reaches the end of the maze, he or she is awarded candy. The entire two-part activity will be done again, this time with the roles reversed and the blindfold placed on the other partner.

When all understand the instructions, distribute a blindfold to each pair. Once the pairs have one member securely blindfolded, invite their partners to quietly scatter to another part of the room or area. Be sure the partners are scattered throughout the area fairly far away from their blindfolded counterparts. When they are in place, invite them to begin calling to their blindfolded partner. The sighted partners must not move from their spot. Encourage them to continue calling until their blindfolded partner touches them.

When all the pairs are united, invite the sighted partners to guide their blindfolded partner to the maze site using only their voice. At the maze, send the pairs through one at a time making sure each pair is separated by approximately five yards. Encourage the sighted partners to walk backward slowly, carefully watching their blindfolded partner's feet while giving voice instructions. If a pair is moving too slowly, ask them to pause and allow the next pair to pass. Remember to keep an eye on their feet to enforce the backward-step rule for those stepping off the path. As each pair finishes, reward the blindfolded youth with candy. When all have finished, return to the beginning area and repeat the activity with the pair reversing roles.

Supply List

- ☐ blindfolds for half of the youth
- ☐ masking tape
- ☐ award candy

Reflection

Read aloud John 10:1–10, John 10:11–18, or John 10:27–30.

Questions for Discussion

☐ What did the activity have to do with the Gospel?

☐ In the Gospel, what image did Jesus use to describe himself?

☐ What do you suppose Jesus was trying to communicate about himself by using this image?

☐ How would you describe God's love for us in this Gospel?

☐ In the activity, how did it feel to help your blindfolded partner through the maze?

☐ When you were blindfolded, how did it feel to know that your partner was in front of you guiding you through the maze?

☐ Who are some of the people who have loved you with this type of shepherd's love in your life?

☐ In the Gospel, what image did Jesus use to describe his followers?

☐ What do you suppose Jesus was trying to say about people by using the sheep analogy?

☐ What are some of the needs God fulfills for people?

☐ What do you suppose Jesus is trying to say about trusting God?

☐ In the Gospel, Jesus speaks of how the sheep recognize the shepherd's voice. How did you feel in the activity as you tried to find your partner by recognizing his or her voice?

☐ What are some ways you recognize and follow God's voice?

☐ What are some of the challenges you face as you try to listen to God's voice?

☐ The Gospel speaks of the shepherd knowing his sheep. How do you feel about a God who knows everything about you yet still loves you unconditionally?

☐ What have you discovered from this Gospel and how can you apply it in your life?

☐ In the next few days, what are some ways you can imitate God's shepherd love?

Catechumenate Connection

This Sunday's Gospel provides a wonderful opportunity to discuss God's love for us and our response to that love. Invite the youth to reflect upon their spiritual journey. How have they experienced God's love? Through whom in their life have they felt guidance, gentleness, compassion, and safety? How have they heard God's voice in their life? Let them articulate how their spiritual journey is a response to this call. Where do they see God leading them?

Invite the youth to read section 754 from the *Catechism of the Catholic Church*. Who are the human shepherds of the church? Discuss the sacrament of holy orders. Explore the roles of bishops, priests, and deacons. What image does the term *pastor* bring to mind? Invite them to reflect on the symbolism of the church as Jesus' flock.

Affirm the youths' desire to know God more deeply. How can they become more attentive to God's voice? What does it mean to know God? How does knowing God change their life?

5th Sunday of Easter (A)

Faith   ✝   *Discipleship*

Readings

Acts 6:1–7
Psalm 33:1–2, 4–5, 18–19
1 Peter 2:4–9
John 14:1–12

Theme

Read John 14:1–12. Jesus in this passage prepares the disciples for his imminent departure and comforts them with the assurance that one day they will dwell together in the Father's house. This place of unity must be prepared first and requires Jesus to leave his friends.

Jesus speaks also of knowing the way to this special place: "I am the way and the truth and the life. No one comes to the Father except through me. If you know me, then you will also know my Father." Jesus' life was an example of how to live in unity with the Father. His compassion for the poor and lowly, his acceptance of sinners, his life of service and prayer, his willingness to let truth lead him through death, these are the ways of one who knows God.

Yet, Philip, like so many people today, simply needed to see God in order to believe. Jesus knew well this human need and invited Philip to look with different eyes, to open his heart, and to sense God's presence in how he had lived. We, too, can look for God with different eyes. Where do we experience mercy and compassion in our lives? Who are those whose lives are dedicated to truth, who seem to courageously follow their inner calling? Where in the community do you find the humble, the open, the trusting people who really believe? Who is it that cares more about you than about what you have accomplished? Are these not examples of God's presence working through people?

This Fifth Sunday of Easter we are called to place our faith in Jesus' message, to trust in his ways of love and mercy, and to sense the good that flows from a life of truth. We are called to imitate Christ and become a sign of God's love to all.

In exploring the Gospel, ask the youth to imagine how the disciples must have felt learning that Jesus was to leave them. Invite the youth to explain what Jesus meant by this dwelling place he had to prepare in his Father's house.

Jesus spoke of how he is the way to the Father. How would the youth describe what Jesus meant by this? What did Jesus mean when he said, "If you know me, then you will also know my Father?" What are some ways Jesus showed he was close to his Father?

Philip asked Jesus, "Master, show us the Father, and that will be enough for us." Why do the youth think Philip asked this? How did Jesus reveal the Father to Philip? What did Jesus mean when he said, "I am in the Father and the Father is in me?" What are some examples of how people's actions reveal God inside them? What did Jesus do in his life that showed us how we should live? What are some ways we are imitating Jesus in our lives and do God's work?

Activity Summary

This activity provides experiences that parallel the main images in this Gospel. The idea is to let the youth discover how closely patterning their life upon Christ's teaching can lead them to a closer union with God. Both faith and actions will be emphasized in the activity. They will also gain insights into how a close relationship with God can affect a person's actions. The activity can also be used to embark on a discussion of how God works through people in diverse ways. Finally, they will experience something of what it is like to have a special place prepared just for them.

The activity is a game that tests the youth's ability to follow directions. A course is laid out with start and finish lines. Each round the leader will choose a card stating a way or method for the youth to run the course. The leader will then demonstrate this method by running the course in the way described on the card. When finished, the leader will choose several youth to imitate his or her actions by running the course in the described manner. As the youth finish, they will be escorted to a cozy area known as Cloud Nine. Here a place will be prepared for each youth where they can enjoy snacks and refreshments and cheer on the rest of the youth. Play continues until all youth are escorted to Cloud Nine.

Bridging the Activity and Reading

☐ The leader in the activity represents Jesus in the Gospel.

☐ The leader preparing a place in Cloud Nine for each person and taking each person there after the race represents Jesus telling the disciples he must go and prepare a place for them and his promise that he would return to take them there.

☐ The leader demonstrating the method for running the course symbolizes the example of Jesus' as the way and the truth and the life.

☐ Running the course in the way demonstrated by the leader represents the life of faith described in the Gospel, "Whoever believes in me will do the works that I do."

Preparation

Begin by choosing a site for the activity. Select a site large enough to accommodate a refreshment area and a racecourse. A gymnasium, large meeting room, or an area outside all work well. First, create the refreshment site known as Cloud Nine. Using masking tape, mark an area large enough to accommodate all the youth comfortably. If an outside site is used and the weather is warm, choose a shaded area for Cloud Nine. The point here is to make this space desirable and cozy. Place a card table in the center of the area and arrange on it a variety of treats, perhaps lemonade, popcorn, and a bowl of candy. Include plates, napkins, cups, and a sign welcoming them to Cloud Nine. Finally, gather a chair, pillow, or mat for each youth and place these in a pile just outside Cloud Nine.

Next, prepare the racecourse. Choose a site in full view of Cloud Nine. Create a starting line by placing masking tape on the floor or ground. The starting line should be long enough to permit several youth to run the course together. Place a finish line, parallel to the starting line, ten to twenty yards away.

Finally, prepare several index cards to be used with the racecourse. On each card, write a different way or method to run the course. Examples include crawling, skipping, hopping like a bunny, walking like a duck, or running backward. Remember, each method will be performed first by the leader in front of the group, so be sure the leader is capable of performing each method. One card will be used each round and rounds will typically last five or six minutes. Consider the number of youth in your group and the amount of time for the activity when planning how many cards to prepare.

With these arrangements in place, you are now ready to introduce the activity. Take the group to the site and show them the starting and finish lines and the area known as Cloud Nine. Announce that they will be tested on how well and how quickly they can follow directions. Explain that each round the leader will prepare a special place in Cloud Nine for those who will be chosen. The leader will then choose a card and read aloud the directions for running the course. Next, the leader will demonstrate the method by running the course as described on the card. When finished, several youth will be chosen to run the course from the starting line to the finish line in the manner written on the card. Those who imitate the leader well and finish the course as described will be escorted to Cloud Nine where they can enjoy comfort and treats for the rest of the activity time. Several rounds will be played so everyone will get a chance to run the course.

When everyone understands, begin the activity by preparing a few places in Cloud Nine. For instance, if you want to choose three youth to run in the first round, take three chairs, pillows, or mats from the pile and arrange them nicely around the table or in a circle within Cloud Nine. When finished, invite all of the youth to gather in an area on the opposite side of the course from Cloud Nine. Shuffle the index cards, and chose one at random. Announce to the group the method listed on the card and demonstrate it by running the course accordingly. Begin behind the starting line, and show the youth the technique, going all the way to the finish line. Next, randomly choose the appropriate number of youth to run the course. If possible, plan on choosing at least two youth for each round. Invite the chosen participants to line up behind the starting line, and copy the leader's technique. Remain behind the finish line, cheering and encouraging the youth.

After the event, congratulate the participants on a job well done. Announce that these youth will be permitted to Cloud Nine. Making an elaborated demonstration, escort the participants to Cloud Nine. Humming "Hail to the Chief" adds pomp and circumstance to this regal event. Upon arriving at Cloud Nine, invite them to lemonade and other treats.

When they are comfortably settled, ask them to watch the next race, cheering on the remaining youth.

Continue each round in the same manner until everyone has had a chance to run the course. Keep those in Cloud Nine involved in the activity by inviting them to cheer for the remaining youth and making them feel welcome when they arrive. It will be important to permit into Cloud Nine only those who finished the course. Be sure to add more refreshments from time to time if needed. Also, do not be in a hurry to move on to the reflection once the last group has entered Cloud Nine. Allow enough time for all the youth to enjoy the refreshments and socializing, and then move the group to the place for reflection.

In any activity where youth are invited to perform, it is possible that one or more may elect not to participate. Be prepared during the activity and in the reflection to handle this situation. If a chosen youth refuses to run the course, consider leaving his or her special place intact, but do not escort that individual to Cloud Nine. Continue with the next round, and consider choosing the individual again. Making several invitations to run the course might convey something of God's mercy. However, if other issues are present, the best choice may be to minimize attention to the matter. Inviting this individual into Cloud Nine at the end of the activity may communicate God's unconditional love.

Supply List

- [ ] prepared index cards
- [ ] masking tape
- [ ] one chair, pillow, or mat for each youth
- [ ] card table
- [ ] treats such as lemonade, popcorn, and candy
- [ ] plates, napkins, and cups
- [ ] "Welcome to Cloud Nine" sign

Reflection

Read aloud John 14:1–12.

Questions for Discussion

- [ ] What did the activity have to do with the Gospel?
- [ ] How do you suppose the disciples felt knowing Jesus was going to leave them?
- [ ] What are some typical things that trouble people your age?
- [ ] How do you suppose the disciples felt knowing Jesus was going to prepare a special place for each of them in his Father's house?
- [ ] In the activity, how did you feel being escorted to your special place in Cloud Nine?
- [ ] In the activity, what did you have to do in order to be escorted into Cloud Nine?
- [ ] How did the leader's actions help you succeed?
- [ ] Why is it easier when you have an example to follow?

☐ What did Jesus mean when he said he is the way to the Father?

☐ How was Jesus' life an example for showing us how to live?

☐ Give an example of a way that Jesus showed love.

☐ In your own life, what are some ways someone has shown you love, or you have shown others love?

☐ What did Jesus mean when he said, "If you know me, then you will also know my Father?"

☐ Why did Philip ask Jesus to show them the Father and that would be all they needed?

☐ What sort of things or examples do you need to see in order to build your faith?

☐ What did Jesus mean when he said, "I am in the Father and the Father is in me?"

☐ If someone had dropped by in the activity when you were running the course without having seen or heard the leader, how could that person know the correct way to run?

☐ What are some examples of how people's actions reveal God inside them?

☐ How does following Christ's example lead a person closer to God?

☐ As a person becomes closer to God, how might that person's actions change?

☐ In the activity there were several different ways or methods for running the course. What are some of the different ways God works through people today?

☐ What have you discovered from this Gospel and how can you apply it in your life?

☐ In the next few days, what can you do to imitate Jesus and let God work through you?

Catechumenate Connection

The Gospel this week gives ample opportunity to discuss and reflect on the word *faith*. Begin by looking up faith in a dictionary. Discuss the definition. Ask the youth why proof is not needed in matters of faith. What do the youth believe about God? How have they come to believe these things?

Invite the youth to look in the Subject Index of the *Catechism of the Catholic Church* and count how many sections refer to faith. What does this say about the importance of faith? Invite them to read aloud one or two of the sections and discuss its meaning.

Catholics are fond of proclaiming their faith with creeds. Distribute copies of the Apostles' Creed. Invite the youth to slowly read each section aloud and discuss the meaning. Next, distribute copies of the Nicene Creed. Again, invite the youth to slowly read each section and discuss the meaning. How are the two creeds similar? How are they different? For background information on the creeds, ask the youth to look up sections 194 and 195 in the *Catechism of the Catholic Church*.

5th Sunday of Easter (B)

Faith   ✝   *Discipleship*

Readings

Acts 9:26–31
Psalm 22:26–27, 28, 30, 31–32
1 John 3:18–24
John 15:1–8

Theme

Read John 15:1–8. Jesus uses beautiful imagery in this passage to communicate the importance of remaining close to God. It is easy to imagine the similarities between the life-giving sap running through the vine and God's life-giving Spirit spreading into each person with love. And just as the vine's sap produces fruit in the branches, so, too, does the Holy Spirit produce good works through those who are open. Jesus is urging his disciples to keep alive within themselves the message he has entrusted to them. Only by remaining in him can they bear the fruit of the Spirit and glorify God.

We, too, are called this Fifth Sunday of Easter to remain in Jesus, to allow his Spirit to nourish us and bring forth fruit. But, these fine words are much easier to say than to do. How do we remain close to Jesus, to keep his Spirit alive within us? What does it mean to bear fruit and how is that done? True enthusiasm for God's work is such a powerful thing. It requires openness to the Spirit of God dwelling within each of us; it seeks the goodness in others and draws it out with a compassion and enthusiasm for all people. Enthusiasm is nourished by remaining close to God through Scripture, prayer, and an eye for God's presence in the many ordinary places of life. It is not enough to simply go through the motions. We are invited to come alive with passion and zeal, to let go of ourselves, and to allow the Spirit to flow through all of our life.

In exploring the reading, invite the youth to describe the analogy Jesus was creating using the image of the vine and branches. Who are the vine grower, the vine, and the branches? What does the fruit represent and who would the sap be? What does Jesus mean when he says the branches are pruned so they will bear more fruit? Ask the youth for examples of activities in their lives that become more important to them than staying connected with God. How can they keep their activities pruned in order to keep their relationship with God the highest priority?

Jesus tells the disciples to remain in him and he will remain in them. Ask the youth to explain this. How do people remain close to God? What are some ways people show they are close to God? What are some examples of fruit we bear because we remain close to God? Ask the youth why Jesus said, "Without me you can do nothing."

Jesus mentioned that people who do not remain in him would wither. Ask the youth for examples of how people wither spiritually when they close themselves off from God. He also said, "If you remain in me and my words remain in you, ask for whatever you want and it will be done for you." Invite the youth to discuss what this means.

Activity Summary

This activity is designed to bring out the symbolism of vine and branches Jesus uses in this Gospel. The youth will experience interdependence and the need to remain connected with one another. This experience should serve to bridge the themes of remaining connected with God and how the Spirit empowers us to bear fruit in the world.

The activity begins with a basket of candy bars situated out of reach from the youth who are to remain behind a line. They are then challenged to figure out a way to get to the candy while adhering to the rules. The rules are simple: Youth may cross over the line toward the candy as long as they remain physically connected to at least one person who is behind the line. Anytime a person is disconnected from the line, he or she must return immediately to the area behind the line. Also, only one candy bar can be taken by a single youth. In time they will figure out that forming a human chain is the way to reach the candy. They must then cooperate, placing different youth at the end each time so everyone has a turn to get a candy bar.

Bridging the Activity and Reading

☐   The chain formed in the activity symbolizes the vine Jesus described in the reading.
☐   Remaining physically connected to others in the chain represents remaining in Christ.
☐   The candy bars symbolize the good works produced by those who remain in Christ.
☐   Being forced to return behind the line if disconnected from the chain represents those who wither if they do not remain in Christ.

Preparation

Preparation is simple. Fill a basket or bowl with candy bars. One bar will be needed for each youth. Next, calculate the amount of space needed by multiplying the number of youth in the group by five feet, six inches. Find a site that will accommodate this distance. A long hallway, gymnasium, or parking lot should work nicely. Prepare the site by placing a masking tape line approximately three feet in length on the floor or ground near one end of the area. Be sure to allow enough space behind the line for all the youth to gather comfortably.

The final step is to place the basket of candy at the precise location. Beginning at the tapeline, measure the distance calculated by multiplying the number of youth by five feet, six inches. Place the basket of candy bars at this point. This step should be done just before the activity begins to insure the accuracy of the headcount and measurement. The idea is to have the candy placed at a point that can only be reached when all the youth work together to form a chain. Be prepared to move the candy closer or further once the first chain is formed. The precise placement is critical.

With these preparations in place, you are now ready to introduce the activity to the group. Explain that the object is for each youth to take a single candy bar from the basket. Anyone able to do so while following all the rules will be allowed to keep their candy bar.

The rules are as follows: First, each youth is allowed to grab only one candy bar. Second, no one except the leader is allowed to move the basket or bowl; it must remain in the exact location it is placed by the leader. Third, players may cross over the line toward the candy as long as they remain physically connected to at least one person who is behind the line. Anytime a person is disconnected from the line, he or she as well as all others linked to him or her must return immediately to the area behind the line. Invite the youth to imagine the area between the masking tape and the candy bars as a vast sea. The masking tape marks the beginning of dry land. Any youth who is not connected to another youth on the land will drown. Fourth, a player's candy bar is not secure until he or she has returned behind the masking tape line while remaining connected to others. If such a player should become disconnected before returning, he or she will surrender the candy bar and begin again.

When all understand, begin the activity. Allow the youth to figure out that forming a human chain is the only way to get the candy. Also allow them to find efficient ways to place a different youth as the candy grabber at the end of the chain. Encourage their efforts, and be sure to watch for violations of the rules. When all youth have successfully obtained a candy bar, move the group to the reflection area.

Supply List

- ☐ basket or bowl
- ☐ one candy bar for each youth
- ☐ masking tape

Reflection

Read aloud John 15:1–8.

Questions for Discussion

- ☐ What did the activity have to do with the Gospel?
- ☐ In the reading, who was represented by the vine grower, the vine, and the branches?
- ☐ If we were to carry this analogy further, whom would the sap represent?
- ☐ Jesus talks about the branches bearing fruit. What does this fruit symbolize?
- ☐ What does Jesus mean when he says the branches are pruned so they will bear more fruit?
- ☐ What activities in your life become more important than staying connected with God?
- ☐ How can you keep your activities pruned in order to keep your relationship with God the highest priority?

☐ In the activity, what did remaining connected allow you to do?

☐ Jesus told the disciples to remain in him and he will remain in them. Why do you suppose this is so important?

☐ How do people remain close to God?

☐ What are some ways people show they are close to God?

☐ What are some examples of fruit that we can bear if we remain close to God?

☐ In the activity how did you feel when you were able to reach a candy bar?

☐ How do you feel in life when you are able to genuinely help someone or show another person love?

☐ What did Jesus mean when he said, "Without me you can do nothing"?

☐ In the activity, what happened to those who became disconnected from the chain?

☐ Jesus mentioned that people who do not remain in him would wither. What are some examples of how people wither spiritually when they close themselves off from God?

☐ Jesus also said, "If you remain in me and my words remain in you, ask for whatever you want and it will be done for you." What does this mean?

☐ What have you discovered from this Gospel and how can you apply it in your life?

☐ In the next few days, what specific things can you do to become more connected with God?

Catechumenate Connection

Invite the youth to read and quietly reflect on John 15:4. Ask them what they can do each day to remain close to God? Why would these actions keep them close to God?

Encourage the youth to discuss prayer. What qualifies as a prayer? When and where can they pray? What is the difference between a prayer from the heart and going through the motions of prayer? How can they make common prayers such as the Our Father more meaningful and simply not routine?

Invite the youth to read section 2742 of the *Catechism of the Catholic Church*. What does it mean to pray without ceasing? What would it mean to be in constant communication with God? How can their words, actions, and thoughts be prayers to God? How would thinking of their lives as a constant prayer influence their words, thoughts, and actions?

Finally, invite the youth to read section 2745 from the *Catechism of the Catholic Church*. Why are prayer and a Christian life inseparable? In today's reading, what did Jesus say would happen to those who become separated from God? What specific ways can the youth increase the quality of their prayer life?

5th Sunday of Easter (C)

Love   ✝

Readings

Acts 14:21–27
Psalm 145:8–9, 10–11, 12–13
Revelation 21:1–5a
John 13:31–33a, 34–35

Theme

Read John 13:31–33a, 34–35. An amazing thing happens in this short Scripture passage. Jesus cuts through the complexity of Jewish law and captures the heart of his teaching with the simple command to love one another. While Moses first introduced this command in Leviticus, the requirement then was to extend love only to one's countrymen and neighbors. Here, Jesus takes love to a new level. He speaks of love as something to be shared and extended to all people. Love is to become a way of life, a living force that defines what it means to be Christian. Also amazing is the context in which this commandment is given. Judas had just left the supper table to prepare his betrayal of Jesus. At a moment when most people would be absorbed in worry, anger, or fear, Jesus takes the opportunity to speak with his disciples of love.

Jesus is not concerned with pretty words or sentiments here. He is commanding the disciples to open themselves to love, lose themselves in its power, and let it take control of their actions. Not only does Jesus speak of love at a time when betrayal is imminent, he offers his life as a template of how it is done: "As I have loved you, so you also should love one another." In letting love take control of our actions, we become true followers of Christ. This Fifth Sunday of Easter we are all called to open ourselves to this way of loving.

When exploring the text with the youth, consider taking a moment to explain the context of this passage. Remind them that Judas had just left to betray Jesus. Invite the youth to explore how they might have felt in a similar situation. How did Jesus' death glorify God? Ask the youth why Jesus told the disciples he would only be with them a little while longer.

Jesus commanded the disciples to love one another. Ask the youth why they suppose love was so important to Jesus. How would the youth describe love? Let them explain some of the different ways people express love. How does the love of a mother differ from the love of a friend? What does it mean to be in love?

Jesus said, "As I have loved you, so you also should love one another." Invite the youth to give examples of how Jesus loved people. What were some ways people responded to the love Jesus showed them? How did Jesus' love change the world?

Jesus told the disciples that their love would be a sign to all that they are Christ's disciples. Ask them what love reveals about a person? How would the youth describe the feeling of love? What are some ways the youth have experienced love in their lives? How does love spread among people? What effect does love have on people? What is required in order to become loving?

Activity Summary

This activity is designed to let the youth experience the different faces of love and how these loving attitudes can be chosen freely. Using puppets they will see and hear how the many subtleties of voice, action, and words can convey a person's attitude and disposition. They will also experience something of the way love takes over a person's actions and the transforming quality of love. The idea is to let the youth discover the diversity of love, its power to transform, and ways to recognize it in their life.

The activity begins with the youth divided into small groups. Each youth will be given a card describing a quality of heart such as irritability, anger, helpfulness, or perhaps kindness. Half of the quality-of-heart cards distributed to any given group will be examples of love. The youth will then be given materials to create a hand puppet and asked to design a puppet in a way that expresses or symbolizes the quality of heart on his or her card. Next, each small group will develop a puppet skit to be performed in front of the large group. The point of these skits is to let the youth express through actions, words, and attitudes the quality of heart describing the puppets. Each skit will be followed by a brief discussion and an opportunity for the youth in the audience to guess the quality of heart of the characters based on what they observed.

Bridging the Activity and Reading

☐ The loving actions of the puppets symbolize the love Jesus commanded the disciples to share with one another.

☐ The audience can tell which puppets act lovingly in the skit. Likewise, in the Gospel, Jesus told the disciples all will know they are his followers because of the love they have for one another.

☐ The puppets in the activity are completely filled with the attitude or disposition of its puppet master. In the same way, Jesus in the Gospel commands the disciples to be completely filled with the same love he has shown them.

Preparation

Begin by gathering an index card for each youth. On each card, write a word that describes a quality of heart such as irritable, petty, helpful, friendly, happy, or angry. Half of these cards should describe some example or expression of love such as kind, caring, or joyful, while the other half can be anything. It is okay to duplicate some of the qualities. Next, gather a lunch bag for each youth and markers, the supplies necessary for simple lunch bag puppets. Finally, prepare the stage area by placing a long table in front of the room. Cover the front of the table completely by draping a tablecloth or blanket over it. The idea is to conceal the puppet masters during the performance.

You are now ready to introduce the activity. Divide the youth into groups of three to five, placing at least one youth with an outgoing personality in each group. Invite the groups to gather at separate tables or areas of the room. Announce that each group will have an opportunity to test their creativity by developing and performing a puppet show for the rest of the youth. The first step is to create a puppet using lunch bags and markers. Demonstrate how a puppet can be quickly created by keeping the bag folded, drawing the eyes on the bottom rectangle of the bag (which is positioned as the top of the puppet), and drawing the mouth on the fold. By inserting a hand inside the bag and placing one's fingers over the inside fold, the puppet's mouth can move when it speaks.

After demonstrating this technique, announce that each youth will also receive an index card. Written on the card is a word to describe the type of puppet to create. These are words that capture something about a person's attitude, disposition, or quality of heart. The idea is to make the puppet appear in such a way that this attitude or disposition is recognizable. For instance, if the word sad appears on the card, a large frown on the puppet's face might be a way to show the disposition.

Once everyone understands the directions for this first step, distribute the lunch bags, markers, and prepared index cards. Be sure each group has at least one or two cards with a loving quality of heart. Invite the youth to begin drawing their puppet, challenging them to be as creative as possible.

When the puppets are finished, announce to the group that it is time to begin the second step. Invite each group to work together to make up a simple play using their puppets. The idea of the play is to use words, actions, and attitudes to demonstrate the quality of heart of each puppet without actually saying the word on the card. Invite them to come up with clever ways the puppets can interact in order to reveal each puppet's disposition. Remind the youth to include a speaking part for each puppet in the group. Show them the stage area and explain how they will be able to sit under the table-stage unseen while performing with their puppets. When everyone understands these step-two directions, announce the allotted time for preparing and rehearsing their play and have them begin.

If a group struggles with a plot, be ready to give suggestions. Invite them to consider a plot centered on everyday events such as studying as a group for a test, getting ready for a party, or a typical religious education session. Keep an eye on the time. Balance preparation and performance time while also leaving adequate time for discussion.

When it is time for the plays to begin, ask if any group would like to perform first. Lead the puppet masters to the area behind the table, and invite the audience to sit in front of the stage.

After the play, invite the puppet masters to walk to the front of the stage for a round of applause. Discuss the play briefly, and ask if anyone in the audience can identify the word on the index card to describe any of the puppets. To keep the discussion lively, consider tossing small candy to any youth with a correct answer. Invite the youth to discuss which puppets demonstrated loving qualities and why these qualities are loving.

Next, ask for another group to volunteer to perform their play. Again, after the performance, discuss the play and invite the audience to guess the word used to describe each puppet. Toss candy for correct answers. Continue until all the groups have had the opportunity to perform. Consider tossing an additional piece of candy to each youth for being good audience participants. Another fun idea is to award candy for the most creative play, the funniest play, the best acting, and so forth. Lead the youth to the discussion area when finished.

Supply List

- ☐ prepared index cards
- ☐ meeting table
- ☐ blanket or tablecloth
- ☐ lunch bags
- ☐ markers
- ☐ small pieces of wrapped candy

Reflection

Read aloud John 13:31–33a, 34–35.

Questions for Discussion

- ☐ What did the activity have to do with the Gospel?
- ☐ Where were Jesus and the disciples and what were they doing when Judas left them?
- ☐ Why did Judas leave them?
- ☐ How do you think Jesus felt when Judas left?
- ☐ How do you feel when people betray you?
- ☐ How did Jesus' life and death glorify God?
- ☐ Why did Jesus tell the disciples he would only be with them a little while longer?
- ☐ Why do you suppose love was so important to Jesus that he commanded the disciples to love?
- ☐ How would you describe love?
- ☐ In the activity, what were some ways the puppets acted lovingly?
- ☐ What are some different ways people express their love?
- ☐ How does the love of a mother differ from the love of a friend?

☐ What does it mean to be in love?

☐ Jesus said, "As I have loved you, so you also should love one another." What are some examples of how Jesus loved people?

☐ What were some ways people responded to the love Jesus showed them?

☐ How did Jesus' love change the world?

☐ While you were watching the puppets in the activity, how could you tell what word was used to describe the puppet?

☐ Jesus told the disciples that their love would be a sign to all that they are Christ's disciples. What do people's actions, words, and attitudes reveal about them?

☐ What are some ways you have experienced love in your life?

☐ In the activity your puppet was completely controlled by you and the attitude you were trying to portray. What must we do to let love completely control our lives?

☐ How does love spread among people?

☐ What effect does love have on people?

☐ How would you describe the feeling of love?

☐ What are some ways you can choose to be loving?

☐ What have you discovered from this Gospel and how can you apply it in your life?

☐ In the next few days, what can you do to reflect God's love more openly to all?

Catechumenate Connection

Invite the youth to reflect on the word *love*. Discuss how others have shown them love. How have they given love? What would it mean to love as Jesus loves? Who does Jesus love and why? What makes some people more lovable than others? Why are Christians called to love all people? How does the church reflect the love of Jesus? In what ways does the church show love to all people? How have they felt God's love at Mass?

Invite the youth to look up the word *charity* in the dictionary. How are charity and love related? Read aloud section 2013 from the *Catechism of the Catholic Church*. How can they devote themselves to the glory of God? How did Jesus devote himself to God's glory? Who exactly is their neighbor? How can they show God's love to all those difficult neighbors at school?

6th Sunday of Easter (ABC)

Faith   ✝   *Love*

Readings

A	B	C
Acts 8:5–8, 14–17	Acts 10:25–26, 34–35, 44–48	Acts 15:1–2, 22–29
Psalm 66:1–3, 4–5, 6–7, 16, 20	Psalm 98:1, 2–3, 3–4	Psalm 67:2–3, 5, 6, 8
1 Peter 3:15–18	1 John 4:7–10	Revelation 21:10–14, 22–23
John 14:15–21	John 15:9–17	John 14:23–29

Theme

Read John 14:15–21, John 15:9–17, or John 14:23–29. This Sixth Sunday of Easter, Jesus has a simple message, "If you love me, you will keep my commandments." In the Year B Gospel he says, "If you keep my commandments, you will remain in my love," and in Year C, he expresses it by saying, "Whoever loves me will keep my word … ." Each of these readings makes it clear that our love for Christ must be shown through our actions and willingness to keep his commandments. And what are these commandments? This, too, Jesus states simply in the Year B Gospel, "This is my commandment: love one another as I love you." So this week we are challenged to grow in our love and express this love to all people through our actions.

A second theme also emerges from these Gospels. In Year A and C, Jesus speaks of "the Advocate, the Holy Spirit" whom the Father will send to be with them to teach and remind them of Jesus' word. This divine presence is also alluded to in the Year B Gospel as Jesus speaks of remaining in the Father's love and the disciples' status as friends instead of slaves. The Holy Spirit's presence in our lives enables us to remain in God's love and extend this love to all people. God's spirit is one of truth and peace, a truth and peace that are beyond worldly comprehension. Only by turning to the Spirit, opening ourselves to the Spirit's presence, and letting the Spirit take charge of our lives, can we truly be transformed into instruments of God's love. This Sixth Sunday of Easter we are also called to open ourselves to God's Spirit and become transformed in love.

In exploring the Gospel with the youth, invite them to discuss why Jesus asked the disciples to keep his commandments. How did keeping his commandments prove their love for Jesus? What were these commandments Jesus wanted the disciples to keep? Ask the youth to describe examples of what it means to love one another. How can these loving actions change people?

Jesus promised to remain close to those who keep his commandments. If Year A or C Gospels are used, focus on how Jesus speaks of sending the Holy Spirit. How do the youth feel knowing God is always with them? Invite them to discuss the role of the Holy Spirit. How does the Holy Spirit help people become more loving? Why do people have trouble accepting the Holy Spirit?

In the Year B Gospel, Jesus says keeping the commandment will let people remain in his love. How do the youth feel knowing that God is always with them? Invite the youth to discuss the image of Jesus as a friend. What are the qualities of a good friend? What are the responsibilities? How did Jesus show love for his friends? How do they feel God's presence when they act with love toward others?

Activity Summary

This activity features both Jesus' command to love others and the Holy Spirit's role in leading us to more loving ways. The idea is to let the youth discover concrete ways they can act with love and how the Holy Spirit can guide these loving actions. They will also experience something of what it is like to have a helper, a symbol of the Holy Spirit's role as teacher and guide. By following the words of the advocate they will be directed in ways that will lead to fulfillment. Additionally, they will be given an opportunity to experience how God's Spirit can work through community actions.

The activity begins by challenging each youth to find ten valuable tokens. Those able to find all ten will be awarded candy. In order to make it possible to find these tokens, the leader will provide clues to the group. These clues will begin with a simple example of how to express love followed by the place to search for the token. The entire group will listen to the clue and search together for the tokens each round. At each site one token will be available for each youth. Once everyone has successfully returned with a token, the next clue is read and the process begins again. The activity is designed to award everyone candy in the end for successfully finding ten tokens.

Bridging the Activity and Reading

☐ The leader in the activity represents the Holy Spirit in the Gospel (In the Year B Gospel, the leader in the activity represents Jesus' friendship and love remaining in the disciples).

☐ The tokens in the activity symbolize acts of love that Jesus commanded in the Gospel.

☐ The clues and examples of love read by the leader in the activity represent how the Holy Spirit (God's love within us for Year B) teaches, reminds, and empowers us to act with love toward all.

☐ Following the clues and finding the tokens symbolize keeping Jesus' commandment to love.

Preparation

Begin by choosing some type of small, plentiful, and inexpensive token to hide. Marbles, popcorn kernels, poker chips, or pennies work well. Ten tokens will be needed for each youth. Next, identify ten sites throughout the parish facilities to hide the tokens such as meeting rooms, the church library, or outside areas. These ten sites will constitute the ten rounds of searching in the activity. At each site, hide one token for each youth using different hiding places within the site. For instance, if your group has twelve youth and your first site is the parish library, hide twelve tokens throughout the room. Repeat this for each of the ten sites. Pick hiding places where the tokens can be found relatively easily. Too much concealment might cause the youth to leave a big mess in their wake at each site.

The next step is to prepare the clues needed to guide the youth to the ten sites. Each clue needs to be composed of two parts: The first should be a simple example of how youth can demonstrate love to others while the second should direct the group to the next site.

In the first part, examples should be concrete, specific, age-appropriate actions that capture something of the spirit of caring for others. One line-sentences ending with "… is a way to show God's love" work well. Examples include: *Being kind to an unpopular classmate at school is a way to show God's love. Resisting the temptation to gossip or laugh at others is a way to show God's love. Helping a younger brother or sister with homework is a way to show God's love. Sitting with someone who is alone at lunch is a way to show God's love.* The idea is for the youth to realize that love takes on many forms and does not need to be a profound act. Love can mean simply being kind to others. Remember to write a different example for each of the ten clues.

The second sentence in each clue should provide a hint about where to find the next site of hidden tokens. This is a wonderful opportunity to indulge your creative side. Simple rhymes, poems, or prose work nicely. Consider composing the clue in such a way that it reveals something about the site while requiring the youth to make a simple deduction in order to solve it. A little creativity here can add a lot of fun to the activity.

Remember to include two parts to each clue. An example of such a two-part clue could read: *Being kind to an unpopular classmate at school is a way to show God's love. Look for tokens one and all; they are hidden at the end of a long hall.*

With these arrangements in place, you are ready to introduce the activity. Begin by announcing that one token for each youth has been hidden in each site. There are ten different sites throughout the facility. Explain that the object of the activity is for each of them to find ten tokens, one at every site. Those who are successful will be awarded candy. At this point, show the group a sample token so they will be easily identified.

Explain that the activity consists of ten rounds. Each round begins with a clue read aloud to the group. This clue will reveal something about a site where tokens are hidden. They must work together to discover the site. Once the site is discovered, the search is on. Only one token is available for each youth at every site. Therefore, youth can take only one token per round. They can, however, help others find tokens. Encourage them to conduct their search with respect for all property, meaning all items must be handled carefully and neatly returned to their original positions. Once each youth has a token, they will bring them to the leader. The leader will then read the next clue and the second round will commence.

When all understand the directions, begin the activity by reading the first example of love followed by the first clue. Accompany the youth to the site and encourage them to work together as a team. When everyone has found a token, collect the tokens and begin the second round by reading the second example of love and the second clue. Continue until all ten clues have been read, and each youth has found ten tokens. Award candy and lead the group to the reflection area.

Supply List

☐ ten tokens for each youth
☐ candy or candy bar for each youth
☐ prepared clues with examples of love and a hiding place on each

Reflection

Read aloud John 14:15–21, John 15:9–17, or John 14:23–29.

Questions for Discussion

For all three Gospels
☐ What did the activity have to do with the Gospel?
☐ In the Gospel, what did Jesus command his disciples to do?
☐ Why do you suppose Jesus asked the disciples to keep his commandments?
☐ How would keeping his commandments prove their love for Jesus?
☐ What were these commands Jesus wanted the disciples to keep?
☐ What are some examples of what it means to love one another?
☐ What are some ways people have acted with love toward you?
☐ How can loving actions change people?
☐ How would the world be different if everyone acted with love in everything they did?

For Year A and C Gospels
☐ What is an advocate? How does an advocate help people?
☐ In the activity, how was the leader like an advocate?
☐ In the activity, what would have happened if you did not receive any clues?
☐ Jesus talked about sending the Holy Spirit or Advocate. What is the role of the Holy Spirit?
☐ How does the Holy Spirit help people become more loving?
☐ Why do you suppose the world has trouble accepting the Holy Spirit?
☐ How do you feel knowing God is always with you to help and guide you?
☐ What are some ways to listen to the Holy Spirit for guidance?
☐ How can you become more aware of the Holy Spirit in your life?
☐ In the activity, the leader read examples of how to show love to others. What are some ways the Holy Spirit guides you in acting lovingly?

For Year B Gospel

- [ ] Jesus promised that his love would remain in those who love one another. How does remaining close to God help you act with love?
- [ ] Jesus referred to the disciples as his friends and not as slaves. What are some qualities of good friends?
- [ ] What are some responsibilities of friendship?
- [ ] How do you feel knowing Jesus considers you a friend?
- [ ] How did Jesus show love for his friends?
- [ ] How do you feel God's presence when you act with love toward others?

For all three Gospels

- [ ] In the activity, how did following the clue lead you to the token?
- [ ] How does following Jesus' command of love lead us to God?
- [ ] In the activity, what would have happened if you had ignored the clue given by the leader?
- [ ] In your own life, what happens to your relationship with God if you ignore the command to love others?
- [ ] In the activity, how did the actions of others help you in your search for the tokens?
- [ ] How do our loving acts of kindness help others see God?
- [ ] How do you see or experience the presence of God through your community?
- [ ] What have you discovered from this Gospel and how can you apply it in your life?
- [ ] In the next few days, what can you do to let God's love show through your actions?

Catechumenate Connection

This Sixth Sunday of Easter is a wonderful opportunity to discuss the role of the Holy Spirit in our faith. Read aloud sections 733, 734, 735, and 736 from the *Catechism of the Catholic Church*. Ask the youth to describe what is meant by the Holy Spirit pouring God's love into our hearts. How can forgiveness be an act of love? Ask them to share an example of how they might have experienced this presence of the Holy Spirit. How can they deepen their relationship with the Holy Spirit? Invite them to give examples of loving acts that the Holy Spirit might empower us to do.

The Holy Spirit constitutes part of the Trinity, the three persons in one God. Read aloud sections 232, 233, and 234 from the *Catechism of the Catholic Church*. Discuss with the youth the Trinity symbolism of the sign of the cross. Discuss the mystery of three persons in one God. Invite the youth to explain how the Trinity might be understood better using the family as an analogy. Describe how the Holy Spirit is symbolized in Scriptures with the image of a dove. Ask the youth to explain this symbolism and how the dove might represent certain features of the Holy Spirit.

Ascension (ABC)

✝   *Discipleship*   ✝

Readings

A	B	C
Acts 1:1–11	Acts 1:1–11	Acts 1:1–11
Psalm 47:2–3, 6–7, 8–9	Psalm 47:2–3, 6–7, 8–9	Psalm 47:2–3, 6–7, 8–9
Ephesians 1:17–23	Ephesians 1:17–23, Ephesians 4:1–13, or Ephesians 4:1–7, 11–13	Ephesians 1:17–23 or Hebrews 9:24–28; 10:19–23
Matthew 28:16–20	Mark 16:15–20	Luke 24:46–53

Theme

Read Acts 1:1–11. "But you will receive power when the Holy Spirit comes upon you, and you will be my witnesses in Jerusalem, throughout Judea and Samaria, and to the ends of the earth." These are Jesus' final words before ascending into heaven. This ascension marks a time of transition for those who follow Jesus. No longer will he be physically present to them; all that remains are memories of his extraordinary life. But, soon there will be more. The Holy Spirit will come upon them bringing amazing gifts and empowering them to bear witness to Jesus throughout the world.

In celebrating the Ascension we also honor our own times of transition. Before we can say hello, there must first be a goodbye; before we can arrive at a new location, we must first leave the place we are now; before we can grow and mature, we must first leave behind narrower and perhaps safer perspectives. This leaving behind of the familiar can be scary in ways that are similar to a death experience. We may often feel compelled to cling to what we are leaving. At these times the words of the two angels may have meaning for us, "Why are you standing there looking at the sky?" There is work to be done, places to go, people to see. Certainly there was an amazing life awaiting the followers of Christ. They were to be visited by the Spirit on Pentecost and eventually carry on the mission of Christ throughout the world. We, too, have been passed the baton of Christ as we work to reflect God's love to others. Ascension celebrates this passing of the baton to humanity and invites us to dedicate ourselves to bringing Christ's love to all.

In each year of the liturgical cycle, Acts 1:1–11 is the one constant reading on the feast of the Ascension. This constancy and its vivid account of Jesus' ascension make it the reading of choice for this session.

In exploring the reading, invite the youth to discuss why Jesus wanted his followers to remain in Jerusalem to await the Holy Spirit. They also asked Jesus if he was going to restore the kingdom to Israel. What do the youth suppose the disciples were expecting?

Jesus responded by telling them they were to receive the Holy Spirit and become witnesses to all people. Invite the youth to discuss what it means to be a witness for Christ. Ask them for examples of how people witness for Christ. How do they suppose the Holy Spirit helps people be witnesses of Christ?

Jesus was lifted up and taken out of their sight as they looked on. Invite the youth to reflect on how Jesus' followers must have felt watching Jesus depart. Ask the youth to share how they feel when someone they care about must leave. What are examples of new things they have never done before, especially things that seem scary? How do they feel when they have a very difficult task ahead of them? What are some examples of things or attitudes people must leave behind if they are to grow?

Activity Summary

This activity is designed to help the youth reflect upon the transition Jesus' followers faced upon his ascension. Additionally, they will have the opportunity to reflect on the important transitions they face in their own lives. The idea is to let them discover what it means to carry on a vision that unites them with others. They will be able to experience leaving behind another, focusing upon the task at hand, and passing the vision on to another to complete. In this way, they may gain insights into ways Christ's followers throughout history, and even today, carry on his mission.

The activity begins with the youth forming one team, or in the case of big groups perhaps two or more teams. They will be led out to a large circular track or course and challenged to run a relay, passing the baton from one teammate to another. The leader will begin each relay by running the first leg of the course, and handing the baton to the first runner. Teammates are positioned around the course in such a way that everyone runs an equal length of the track. In large groups several laps around the course may be needed. The race is completed once the last runner passes the finish line and hands the baton back to the leader.

Bridging the Activity and Reading

☐ The leader represents Jesus and the runners represent his followers.

☐ The leader passing the baton to the first runner symbolizes Jesus leaving his followers and asking them to be witnesses to the ends of the earth.

☐ Running the course and passing the baton to teammates represents how Christ's followers, filled with the Holy Spirit, continue to be witnesses to him through time.

☐ Returning the baton to the leader at the end of the race symbolizes the angel's prediction that Jesus will return to us.

Preparation

Preparation for this activity is easy. Find a site large enough to accommodate an oval track for a relay. An athletic track circling a football field is ideal. If your facility does not have such a track, a big open area outside will work nicely. If the activity must be held indoors, a gymnasium or large gathering room will also work well. Use masking tape to create a starting line on the floor or ground. Mark the course by placing cones or masking tape along the route if an athletic track is not available. If this activity takes place indoors, consider routing the course near the walls of the room and having the youth walk the relay. The course should be designed as a loop or oval with the starting line also serving as the finish line.

Each of the runners should run an equal distance in the relay. If your track is relatively short, consider making each runner's leg one lap. If you have a larger track, consider how many youth are in the group and divide the course into that many sections. Each section will represent an individual runner's leg of the relay.

Next, find an object to use as a relay baton. The baton should be suitable for holding while running and easy to pass to a teammate. A racing baton designed for track and field events is an ideal choice, although an object such as a paper towel tube will also work.

Finally, estimate the time it will take the group to run this course. Figure the length of each leg, how long it might take a youth to run a single leg, and multiply this time by the number of participants. Add time for the leader to run a leg also. This estimated time will become the challenge you offer the group.

With these preparations in place, you are now ready to introduce the activity. Lead the youth to the prepared track and announce that the entire group will be running a relay as a single team. Explain that the leader will run the first leg of the relay, and pass the baton to the first runner. That youth will run his or her leg of the relay and pass the baton to the next runner. Each runner will run a leg and pass the baton to the next runner until everyone has completed a leg of the relay and the final runner has returned the baton to the leader. Finally, challenge the youth to run the entire course in the allotted time you have determined earlier.

When everyone understands the directions, walk the course with the youth placing them in the locations where they will begin their leg of the race. Consider letting the youth decide among themselves who will run which leg of the course. When all are ready, begin the relay. Run the first leg and pass the baton to the first runner. Continue to cheer for them as they pass the baton to teammates. When the final youth hands the baton back to the leader, stop the clock, announce the time, and congratulate everyone on a job well done. If time allows, announce that the relay will be run again. If they fell short of the goal, adjust the allotted time to make the challenge more attainable. If they beat the goal easily, consider making the allotted time more challenging. It is important that the group experience success at least once. Finally, lead the youth to the reflection area for some well-deserved rest.

Supply List

- ☐ masking tape
- ☐ optional cones to mark the course
- ☐ racing baton
- ☐ stop watch or a watch with a second hand

Reflection

Read aloud Acts 1:1–11.

Questions for Discussion

- ☐ What did the activity have to do with the reading?
- ☐ Why did Jesus want his followers to remain in Jerusalem to await the Holy Spirit?
- ☐ What did his followers expect Jesus to do before he left?
- ☐ Jesus told them they were to receive the Holy Spirit and be his witnesses to all. What did Jesus mean by this?
- ☐ In the activity, what was your team's goal?
- ☐ What was your role in helping your team accomplish the goal?
- ☐ What does it mean to be a witness for Christ?
- ☐ How would you describe the message Jesus wanted spread to all people?
- ☐ How do people today carry on the work of Jesus and pass his message to others?
- ☐ How does the Holy Spirit help people carry on Jesus' mission?
- ☐ In the reading, Jesus was lifted up and left their sight forever. How do you suppose his followers felt once Jesus had left?
- ☐ How do you feel when you must leave someone you really care about?
- ☐ Jesus told his followers to be witnesses to the end of the earth. How do you suppose they felt facing this very difficult task without their leader?
- ☐ What are some things you have never done before, especially things that seem overwhelming, difficult, or scary?
- ☐ How do you feel facing these challenges?
- ☐ In the activity, what did you have to leave behind in order to help your team reach its goal?
- ☐ What would have happened if you had not left the teammate who handed you the baton?
- ☐ What are some examples of things you feel you must leave behind in life in order to grow?
- ☐ What types of important changes do you expect to go through in life?
- ☐ How can the Holy Spirit help you face change with courage and hope?
- ☐ What are some examples of things or attitudes people must leave behind if they are to grow closer to God?
- ☐ In the reading, angels appeared and asked them why they were standing around looking at the sky. What sorts of things help us remain focused on doing God's work?

- ☐ In the activity, how did you feel knowing you helped your team accomplish its goal?
- ☐ How did you know everyone on your team shared the same goal?
- ☐ How can you tell if a person is carrying on the mission of Christ?
- ☐ What have you discovered from this reading and how can you apply it in your life?
- ☐ In the next few days, what can you do to bring God's love to another person?

Catechumenate Connection

Invite the youth to read section 670 from the *Catechism of the Catholic Church*. Discuss with the youth how the church continues the work of Christ here on earth. What are some ways we can see evidence of God's kingdom emerging in our lives? Invite them to discuss various vocational callings and how priests, nuns, monks, married people, single people, and children each have special ways they can pass along God's message of love.

Ascension is a wonderful opportunity to discuss with the youth how the church has undergone transition through time. Provide them with a brief history of the church. Talk about how Christians in the first three centuries were persecuted, how they had to meet in secret to worship and how they risked their own death for their faith. Explore how things dramatically changed for Christians in the fourth century, when the Roman ruler Constantine the Great was converted to Christianity and made it the state religion. Discuss how this transition institutionalized the church and moved her farther from her simple beginnings. If time permits, discuss the various councils, the church's move to Rome, the reformation period, and how Vatican Council II has brought dramatic changes to how our worship is experienced.

7th Sunday of Easter (ABC)

Discipleship   ✝   *Prayer*

Readings

A	B	C
Acts 1:12–14	Acts 1:15–17, 20a, 20c–26	Acts 7:55–60
Psalm 27:1, 4, 7–8	Psalm 103:1–2, 11–12, 19–20	Psalm 97:1–2, 6–7, 9
1 Peter 4:13–16	1 John 4:11–16	Revelation 22:12–14, 16–17, 20
John 17:1-11a	John 17:11b–19	John 17:20–26

Theme

Read John 17:1–26. This Seventh Sunday of Easter, the Gospel takes us back to a moment in Christ's life just before his passion and crucifixion. Here we are able to eavesdrop with the disciples on an intimate moment of prayer between the Father and Son, a moment when Jesus speaks of his departure from earth, his concern for those he leaves behind, and his unity with the Father and all the faithful. As the Easter season draws to a close, it seems appropriate to recall this prayer of Jesus and reflect on how our works of faith and love continue Christ's mission here on earth. In letting the Spirit work through us, we bring God's presence to others and participate in the building of God's kingdom. This willingness to become the arms and legs of God's word, this open response to the call of the Spirit, is a sign of our unity with God.

In the Gospel, Jesus intercedes for the welfare of all those who believe, much as a mother might pray with compassion and concern for the welfare of her children. His prayer, his concern for all, his desire for their well-being is expressed in the moments just before he is to endure a painful death. This outpouring of love in the face of his suffering is a wonderful model for us to follow. If we can reflect this spirit of love into the world, then truly we are builders of the kingdom. To love such as this, however, requires a closeness and unity with God, the source of all love. We, too, must imitate the prayerfulness of Jesus and attend closely to the word of God speaking in our soul. For it is this prayerfulness, this compassion for others, this willingness to do the work of God that truly is the heart of God's kingdom. The world transformed as God wants it to be is the kingdom of God.

The lectionary designers divide this prayer of Jesus' into thirds, placing one part into each of the three years of the liturgical cycle for the Seventh Sunday of Easter. Each year's Gospel features Jesus in prayer, his concern for those he is about to leave behind, and the unity between the Father, the Son, and all the faithful. Consider, however, reviewing the

---

entire prayer (John 17:1–26) with the youth to provide a richer context and deeper experience of this intimate moment with Jesus.

In reviewing the Scripture, begin by explaining that Jesus offered this prayer just before he was to begin his passion and crucifixion. Ask the youth what Jesus seemed to be concerned about in this prayer. How do his concerns differ from what others might be concerned with before facing their death? Why is it important to share our concerns with God?

Invite the youth to discuss how prayers of petition differ from prayers of praise or thanksgiving. What were the various things Jesus asked for in this prayer? How do the youth pray and what are some examples of petitions they might offer?

Jesus speaks about the unity between himself, the Father, and those who believe. Ask the youth for examples of how we as believers might show that we are close to God. Invite the youth to discuss the goal or mission Jesus had while he was on earth. As followers of Christ, how do we help Jesus continue to carry out his mission today?

Activity Summary

This activity is designed to explore the reading from the disciples' perspective. The youth will recognize the need to listen closely to the words of the leader and try to discern their meaning as they attempt to act upon them. Their willingness to create what the leader wants will symbolize the experience of God's word dwelling within the believers. As the vision expressed by the leader unfolds, they will discover they must put aside their competitive ways and work together as one team. Working together to create a pyramid will also speak of their unity with the leader, a symbol of their unity with God.

The activity begins with the youth divided into several teams. They are challenged to do two things: discern what the leader wants by listening to his or her clues and build the object the leader wants. Candy is promised to whoever can meet the challenge first. Plenty of building materials are also provided for their use. Each round the leader gives a short clue that is followed with ample time for the youth to act. After a reasonable time has passed, the leader moves to round two by announcing a second clue. In time it becomes evident that the leader wants a human pyramid to be formed by all the youth in all the groups. Once the youth recognize this and create the pyramid, all are awarded candy.

Bridging the Reading and Activity

- ☐ The leader represents Jesus and the youth represent the disciples listening to Jesus.
- ☐ The clues in the activity symbolize Jesus' prayers of petition.
- ☐ Listening to the clues represents the disciples listening to Jesus as he revealed God's word.
- ☐ Working to create what the leader wanted symbolizes the disciples remaining in the world to carry on Jesus' mission.
- ☐ Building a pyramid of people symbolizes the unity of all that Jesus prayed about.

Preparation

Begin by finding a site large enough to accommodate a human pyramid composed of all the youth in the group. An area outside, a gymnasium, or a large meeting room works nicely. Take precautions to ensure the safety of those who may be positioned toward the top of the pyramid. Consider moving furniture, providing tumbling mats, or simply choosing a site on soft ground. At the appropriate time, be prepared to move the group to this area.

Next, gather a variety of building materials that the youth can use to make different types of structures in the meeting room. Examples include building blocks, Legos, Popsicle sticks, glue, gumdrops, toothpicks, cardboard, and tape. A large assortment of these materials will give the youth many options. You might also consider adding decorative materials such as yarn, popcorn kernels, leaves, marbles, string, playing cards, and wrapping paper to encourage the youth's creativity. Display these materials in a central place in the room. Also, have reserve materials on hand to replenish the supply as needed after each round.

Finally, write the following requests on a piece of paper, keeping them in the correct sequence. Since the leader will speak these requests, only one copy is needed.

1. I want a structure built.
2. I would like the structure to have a foundation.
3. I would like the structure to reach into the air.
4. I would like all the people to work together.
5. I want all groups to be one team.
6. I want the structure in a place I have designated.
7. I want a pyramid made of people.
8. I want to give candy to all the people who form one large pyramid.

With these preparations in place, you are now ready to introduce the activity. Choose your words carefully when explaining the activity to the youth. It is important for them to assume they are competing against other teams. In reality, however, they are one big team simply divided into a number of groups.

Divide the youth into several groups. Announce that the activity will consist of two challenges: first, they must figure out what the leader wants and, second, they must do what the leader wants. The first team to successfully meet these two challenges wins candy. Phrasing the instructions this way should create the desired effect.

Explain that several rounds will be played. Each round the leader will offer a clue about what he or she wants. These clues will be given in the form of a request or petition. The youth must listen carefully to the request and then try to figure out what it is they must do. The leader will give the groups a reasonable amount of time to work with the clue. At this point, show them the materials they are permitted to use in the activity. Explain that if the request is not fulfilled in a reasonable amount of time, the next round will start with another clue or petition. The activity ends once a team completes the request in the exact manner envisioned by the leader.

When all understand, begin by reading the first petition. Allow the groups time to brainstorm and be creative. Keep an eye on the time considering that seven or eight rounds will be needed. If too much time is given each round, the activity may drag. Try to time each round in a way that keeps the activity moving.

Move from group to group offering positive comments without revealing if they are building the structure incorrectly. Be sure not to offer any other clues outside of the written petitions. If a group should ask which building materials to use, remind them that part of the activity is to figure out what the leader wants. After a few minutes, have the leader announce that the structure is not being built according to his or her desires and it is time to move on to the next round. Replenish materials as needed, read the next petition, and invite the groups to begin again.

Once the youth are given the sixth clue, lead them to the designated area. When they realize they need to build a human pyramid, caution them on being safe. Enlist other adults to help with spotting the youth as they are climbing. If there is a large number of youth, encourage them to make the pyramid wider instead of taller for safety reasons. The pyramid should not exceed three youth in height. Congratulate them on a job well done, and award candy to each youth. When finished, move the entire group to the reflection area.

Supply List

- ☐ a large variety of building and decorative materials
- ☐ a list of the petitions for the leader
- ☐ candy

Reflection

Read aloud John 17:1–11a, John 17:11b–19, or John 17:20–26. Another option is to read the entire passage, John 17:1–26, to provide the youth with the complete prayer.

Questions for Discussion

- ☐ What did the activity have to do with the Gospel?
- ☐ Who was Jesus talking to in the Gospel? What must the disciples have been doing while Jesus was praying to God?
- ☐ In the activity, how did you discover what to do?
- ☐ In the Gospel, how did the disciples discover how to carry on Jesus' mission?
- ☐ What did Jesus pray for?
- ☐ Whom did Jesus want united?
- ☐ Why do you think Jesus was concerned about unity for his followers?
- ☐ In the activity, what did you have to figure out to be able to do what the leader wanted?
- ☐ How was your attitude about other groups different at the end of the activity than at the beginning of the activity?
- ☐ Jesus offered this prayer just before he was to begin his passion and crucifixion. What was Jesus concerned about in this prayer?
- ☐ How were Jesus' concerns different from others who might be facing death?
- ☐ What do these concerns and this prayer tell you about what was in Jesus' heart?

- ☐ Why is it important to share our concerns with God?
- ☐ What is the difference between prayers of petition and prayers of praise or thanksgiving?
- ☐ What were the various things Jesus asked for in this prayer?
- ☐ What are some examples of things you ask of God?
- ☐ Besides asking for things, what are some other ways you pray to God?
- ☐ In this prayer, Jesus prays for the well-being of his friends. How do you suppose the disciples felt listening to Jesus pray for them in this way?
- ☐ Jesus spoke of sending his disciples and all believers into the world and how they are one with him and the Father. How do you feel knowing you are united with God?
- ☐ As followers of Christ, how can our actions show that we are close to God?
- ☐ What does it mean to have God's word dwelling within you?
- ☐ How would you describe Jesus' goal or mission while he was on earth?
- ☐ As followers of Christ, how do we help Jesus continue to carry out his mission today?
- ☐ In the activity, how did you know what the leader wanted?
- ☐ In your life, how do you know what God wants for you?
- ☐ What are some ways we can remain close to God in our daily lives?
- ☐ In the activity, how did you change your actions and attitudes as you heard more and more clues?
- ☐ How do people change as they grow closer to God?
- ☐ What have you discovered from this Gospel and how can you apply it in your life?
- ☐ In the next few days, how can you listen more closely to God?

Catechumenate Connection

Explain that the prayer found in John 17:1–26 is called the priestly prayer of Jesus. Ask the youth why they think it has been given this title. Invite them to read sections 2746–2751 of the *Catechism of the Catholic Church*. Why is so much emphasis given to this prayer? Section 2749 states, "Our high priest who prays for us is also the one who prays in us and the God who hears our prayer." What do the youth think this means? What does this statement say about our relationship with God?

Since prayer is the theme this week, explain that there are many common Catholic prayers. Distribute copies of the Our Father, Hail Mary, and Glory Be. Invite the youth to read the words and discuss their meaning. Explain how these are prayed during a devotion called the Rosary. Give a brief history of the Rosary and ask the youth to take turns reading each mystery aloud. After each mystery is read, invite the youth to picture the scene in their mind. Encourage discussion about what they envision.

Pentecost (ABC)

| | Holy Spirit | ✝ | Discipleship | |

Readings

A	B	C
Acts 2:1–11	Acts 2:1–11	Acts 2:1–11
Psalm 104:1, 24, 29–30, 31, 34	Psalm 104:1, 24, 29–30, 31, 34	Psalm 104:1, 24, 29–30, 31, 34
1 Corinthians 12:3b–7, 12–13	1 Corinthians 12:3b–7, 12–13 or Galatians 5:16–25	1 Corinthians 12:3b–7, 12–13 or Romans 8:8–17
John 20:19–23	John 20:19–23 or John 15:26–27, 16:12–15	John 20:19–23 or John 14:15–16, 23b–26

Theme

Read Acts 2:1–11. A sudden loud noise coming from the sky like a strong driving wind; tongues of fire appearing, separating and moving toward each person; amazing powers enabling Spirit-filled people to speak in foreign tongues—these were the dramatic ways the Holy Spirit appeared to those who inherited Christ's mission on earth. What must it have been like to be there and witness the miracle of God's presence among this early church? What must it have been like to be filled with the Holy Spirit and be moved to speak of God in ways that all could understand?

Pentecost Sunday feeds our imagination with images that elevate us out of the ordinary and into the divine. These dramatic and fantastic events engage us and appeal to our need to transcend ourselves, perhaps to go forth into the world and evangelize. In remembering the Spirit's descent upon the church in her infancy, we also reflect on how the Spirit visits each of us with unique gifts today. We may not be able to speak in tongues and communicate with people of all nations, yet if we are open to God's presence we will be empowered with subtle gifts that are very important. Patience, compassion, empathy, sincerity, these, too, are genuine gifts from the Spirit that have a universal power to touch all of humanity. Pentecost invites us to be open to the Spirit, acknowledge the gifts we have been given, discern how God is calling us, and respond with courage to share our gifts.

In each year of the liturgical cycle, Acts 2:1–11 is the one constant reading on Pentecost Sunday. This constancy and its wonderful account of the Holy Spirit's visit make it the reading of choice for this Pentecost session.

In exploring the text, explain to the youth that Jesus had already ascended into heaven but had instructed his followers to remain gathered in Jerusalem to await the Spirit's visit. Invite the youth to discuss what it must have been like to witness the Spirit's visit. How do they suppose the people felt hearing the wind and seeing the tongues of fire? What do they suppose it felt like being filled with the Holy Spirit? What must it have been like to speak in ways that everyone could understand?

The Jews from various nations were amazed when they heard these Spirit-filled people speak in their language. What are some ways God's presence amazes people today? How are they able to recognize God's presence in their lives? Invite the youth to offer examples of gifts the Holy Spirit gives to people. Invite them to discuss ways people use these gifts to spread God's love.

Activity Summary

This activity is designed to parallel the experience of the early Christians on Pentecost. Each youth will be given a gift enabling him or her to accomplish a goal in dramatic fashion. Each youth's response to the gift will be key in allowing the group as a whole to meet its goal. The idea is to let the youth discover that the Spirit's gifts are given freely and these gifts empower them to spread God's love. Also, the activity will allow them to reflect on the importance of responding to these gifts; in using our gifts we contribute to the good of the community.

The activity begins by challenging the youth to run a timed course using only small baby steps. Candy is offered to all who are successful. In round one, the time and distance of the course is designed to make it impossible to meet the challenge. Round two is set up in the same way, but this time the leader explains that a tennis ball may be placed in front of some runners. Those who pick up the ball will be allowed to sprint to the finish line. As runners cross the line, the leader will recycle the ball or balls continuing to place them on the course throughout the entire round. The idea is to let a few of the youth experience this gift. The third round will be run just as the second; however, this time candy is awarded only if the entire group completes the course within the allotted time. Also, the runners, instead of the leader, will be allowed to recycle the balls throughout the course after they cross the finish line. If the group is unsuccessful in round three, a fourth round will be run with adjustments made in order to let the group experience success.

Bridging the Activity and Reading

- ☐ The tennis balls in the activity represent the gifts from the Holy Spirit.
- ☐ Those who are given a tennis ball symbolize those who were given gifts of the Spirit.
- ☐ Running with the tennis ball symbolizes how the early Christians responded to the Holy Spirit by preaching the Good News.
- ☐ In the final round the entire group is successful because everyone shares their gifts. This represents how others heard about God's works because of those who shared their gifts from the Holy Spirit.

Preparation

Begin by choosing an appropriate site for the activity. The site needs to be large enough to accommodate a thirty-yard racecourse and wide enough to allow all of the youth to stand comfortably side-by-side. An area outside, a gymnasium, or a long hallway all work nicely. Create a starting line by placing masking tape on the floor or ground. Be sure to make it long enough to allow all the youth to run simultaneously. Place a finish line parallel to the starting line thirty yards away. Finally, gather one tennis ball for every five youth in the group. If tennis balls are not available, find similar objects the youth can run with safely.

You are now ready to introduce the activity. Lead the group to the prepared site. Explain the object of the activity is to move from the starting line to the finish line in less than two minutes. The challenge, however, is in how the course must be run. Only small sideways baby steps can be used. Announce that candy will be awarded to those who successfully meet this challenge.

At this point, explain and demonstrate the sideways baby-step technique required to run the course. All runners will begin with one shoulder pointed toward the finish line and both feet together. This starting position should resemble a single file line with all runners facing an imaginary sideline. The running technique is more of a sideways walk in which they cross their legs and move one foot-width each step. For example, if a youth's right shoulder is facing the finish line, that youth must cross his or her left leg over the right, placing the left foot so that the outside of it touches the outside of his or her right foot. To take the next step, the youth must uncross his or her legs and place the inside of the right foot next to the inside of the left foot, so that the inside of both feet touch. These two steps are alternated throughout the course. Emphasize that proper technique requires the sides of both feet to touch each step. Those who fail to use proper technique will return to the starting line and begin again.

When all understand, invite the youth to practice the technique for a few minutes. Observe them and be available to help them master the technique. When all are ready, invite the runners to line up behind the starting line. Announce again they have two minutes to run the course and that the sides of their feet must touch at the end of each step. Begin the race. Be sure to watch for violations, as the temptation will be strong to end a step with their feet apart. Escort offenders back to the starting line. Keep in mind that the idea of this first round is to have all the youth fail. It should be impossible to run this thirty-yard course in two minutes using this technique.

At the two-minute mark, call time and ask the youth to stop and return to the starting line. Announce that since no one was successful, there will be another opportunity to win candy. This time, however, the rules will change a bit. Explain that the same sideways baby-step technique will be used; however, the leader will place a tennis ball in front of one or more runners. When this happens, the runner is allowed to pick up the ball and sprint to the finish line. Once the runner crosses the finish line, he or she will immediately give the ball back to the leader, who will then place it in front of another runner. Remind them again that only those with a tennis ball are allowed to sprint; all others must use the sideways baby-step technique.

When all understand, begin the second round. Randomly place one tennis ball in front of a runner. Follow the youth to the finish line, retrieve the ball, and quickly place it in front of another runner. The idea is to have some of the youth win candy because of this gift, while others in the group do not win candy.

After two minutes, call time and invite the youth back to the starting line once again. Give candy to all who crossed the finish line. Expect some protests from those who did not have a tennis ball placed in front of them. Explain there will be a third round of play. Again, as in round two, the youth must use the sideways baby-step technique until they pick up a tennis ball, empowering them to sprint to the finish line. Once at the finish line, however, the youth may sprint back and place their tennis ball in front of another runner of their choice. Candy will only be awarded if the entire group crosses the finish line within two minutes.

When all understand, begin the third round. Place a ball in front of several of the youth. Watch the time, and consider placing additional tennis balls in front of youth as needed. The idea is for the youth to be challenged during this round, but be successful. If they are not successful in this round, play one more round using more tennis balls. When finished, congratulate the group on their success, distribute candy to all, and lead the group to the reflection area.

Supply List

- ☐ masking tape
- ☐ tennis balls
- ☐ stopwatch or watch with a second hand
- ☐ candy

Reflection

Read aloud Acts 2:1–11.

Questions for Discussion

- ☐ What did the activity have to do with the reading?
- ☐ In the activity, how did it feel trying to get to the finish line in round one?
- ☐ For those that were given a tennis ball in round two, how did it feel to be allowed to run?
- ☐ How do you think the disciples felt when they were filled with the Holy Spirit?
- ☐ In rounds two and three, what did you do to earn the gift of the tennis ball?
- ☐ How is this similar to the way the Holy Spirit gives gifts?
- ☐ Although the ball was a gift and you did nothing to earn it, what did you have to do before you could run with it?
- ☐ What must we do in order to use the gifts given to us by the Holy Spirit?
- ☐ How do you suppose the disciples felt being able to speak in other languages?
- ☐ How did they share their gift with others?
- ☐ How did the devout Jews respond to the disciples?

☐ How does God's presence amaze people today?

☐ What are some examples of the gifts the Holy Spirit gives to people today?

☐ How can people use gifts such as compassion, listening, and being a good friend to spread God's love?

☐ In round three of the activity, you had the option of sharing the tennis ball with others, or keeping it for yourself. Why did you share it?

☐ Why do you think the disciples wanted to share their gift?

☐ How would things be different today if the early Christians refused to use the gifts given to them by the Holy Spirit?

☐ In your own life, who are some people you know that have certain gifts or talents and how do they use them to help others?

☐ Why do you think these people share their gifts and talents?

☐ How are others affected by these gifts?

☐ What gifts and talents have you been given?

☐ In what ways can you use your gifts and talents to spread God's love to others?

☐ What have you discovered from this reading and how can you apply it in your life?

☐ In the next few days, what specific ways can you share your gifts and talents?

Catechumenate Connection

Explain to the youth how Pentecost represents the birthday of the church. Invite them to discuss how the Holy Spirit has empowered Christians to continue Jesus' mission on earth. The Holy Spirit is also present in a special way to Christians through the sacraments. Discuss with them how baptism, confirmation, Eucharist, and reconciliation are opportunities to experience the Spirit's presence.

Explain how the Holy Spirit has been described in Scriptures as fire, wind, and even a dove. Invite the youth to envision the Holy Spirit, and discuss what they imagine. What challenges do they find in trying to describe the Holy Spirit? In what ways have they seen or felt the Holy Spirit in their lives? How was the Holy Spirit described in the reading? What effect did the Holy Spirit have on the disciples? How were others touched by the disciples' gift?

The feast of Pentecost gives ample opportunity to discuss many Catholic symbols. Ask the youth to note the color of vestments used at Mass. Why do they suppose the church chose red to be the color for this feast? Invite the youth to read section 696 in the *Catechism of the Catholic Church*. Where have they seen the symbol of fire used at Mass? How can the Holy Spirit transform people in ways similar to how a fire transforms things?

Appendixes

Index of Scripture Passages

Scripture	Sunday	Activity	Page
John 17:1–11a	7th Easter (A)	Structure Dilemma	125
John 17:11b–19	7th Easter (B)	Structure Dilemma	125
John 17:20–26	7th Easter (C)	Structure Dilemma	125
John 20:1–9	Easter Sunday (ABC)	Easter Basket Search	73
John 20:19–31	2nd Easter (ABC)	Discernment by Touching	78
John 21:1–19	3rd Easter (C)	Recognition Game/Party	92
Acts 1:1–11	Ascension (ABC)	Relay Race	120
Acts 2:1–11	Pentecost (ABC)	Gift Race	130

Index of Sessions

Session	Activity	Theme(s)	Page
1st Lent (ABC)	Drink Temptation	Temptation, Perseverance	13
2nd Lent (ABC)	Bermuda Triangle	Conversion, Trust	18
3rd Lent (A)	Treasure Hunt	Seeking God, Discipleship	23
3rd Lent (B)	Justice Skits	Justice	28
3rd Lent (C)	Puzzle Contest	Repentance, Conversion	32
4th Lent (A)	Blind Relay	Faith, Judging Jesus	36
4th Lent (B)	Red Light, Green Light	Faith	41
4th Lent (C)	Race for a Party	Repentance, Forgiveness	45
5th Lent (A)	Freedom Circle	Resurrection, Faith	50
5th Lent (B)	Cookie Bake	Sacrifice, Service	55
5th Lent (C)	Tag Games	Forgiveness	60
Palm Sunday (ABC)	Passion Reflection	Christ's Passion	64
Easter Sunday (ABC)	Easter Basket Search	Resurrection, Faith	73
2nd Easter (ABC)	Discernment by Touching	Faith, Discernment, Gaining Perspective	78
3rd Easter (A)	Paper Bag Mystery	Faith	82
3rd Easter (B)	Charades	Faith	87
3rd Easter (C)	Recognition Game/Party	Recognizing God, Discipleship	92
4th Easter(ABC)	Blindfolded Walk	God's Love, Trust	97
5th Easter (A)	Imitation Course	Faith, Discipleship	101
5th Easter (B)	Candy Bar Grab	Faith, Discipleship	106
5th Easter (C)	Puppet Skits	Love	110
6th Easter (ABC)	Token Search	Faith, Love	115
Ascension (ABC)	Relay Race	Discipleship	120
7th Easter (ABC)	Structure Dilemma	Discipleship, Prayer	125
Pentecost (ABC)	Gift Race	Holy Spirit, Discipleship	130

Cross-Reference by Theme

Theme	Session Plans	Activity	Page
Christ's Passion	Palm Sunday (ABC)	Passion Reflection	64
Conversion	2nd Lent (ABC)	Bermuda Triangle	18
	3rd Lent (C)	Puzzle Contest	32
Discernment	2nd Easter (ABC)	Discernment by Touching	78
Discipleship	3rd Lent (A)	Treasure Hunt	23
	3rd Easter (C)	Recognition Game/Party	92
	5th Easter (A)	Imitation Course	101
	5th Easter (B)	Candy Bar Grab	106
	Ascension (ABC)	Relay Race	120
	7th Easter (ABC)	Structure Dilemma	125
	Pentecost (ABC)	Gift Race	130
Faith	4th Lent (A)	Blind Relay	36
	4th Lent (B)	Red Light, Green Light	41
	5th Lent (A)	Freedom Circle	50
	Easter Sunday (ABC)	Easter Basket Search	73
	2nd Easter (ABC)	Discernment by Touching	78
	3rd Easter (A)	Paper Bag Mystery	82
	3rd Easter (B)	Charades	87
	5th Easter (A)	Imitation Course	101
	5th Easter (B)	Candy Bar Grab	106
	6th Easter (ABC)	Token Search	115
Forgiveness	4th Lent (C)	Race for a Party	45
	5th Lent (C)	Tag Games	60
Gaining Perspective	2nd Easter (ABC)	Discernment by Touching	78
God's Love	4th Easter (ABC)	Blindfolded Walk	97
Holy Spirit	Pentecost (ABC)	Gift Race	130
Judging Jesus	4th Lent (A)	Blind Relay	36
Justice	3rd Lent (B)	Justice Skits	28

Theme	Session Plans	Activity	Page
Love	5th Easter (C)	Puppet Skits	110
	6th Easter (ABC)	Token Search	115
Perseverance	1st Lent (ABC)	Drink Temptation	13
Prayer	7th Easter (ABC)	Structure Dilemma	125
Recognizing God	3rd Easter (C)	Recognition Game/Party	92
Repentance	3rd Lent (C)	Puzzle Contest	32
	4th Lent (C)	Race for a Party	45
Resurrection	5th Lent (A)	Freedom Circle	50
	Easter Sunday (ABC)	Easter Basket Search	73
Sacrifice	5th Lent (B)	Cookie Bake	55
Seeking God	3rd Lent (A)	Treasure Hunt	23
Service	5th Lent (B)	Cookie Bake	55
Temptation	1st Lent (ABC)	Drink Temptation	13
Trust	2nd Lent (ABC)	Bermuda Triangle	18
	4th Easter (ABC)	Blindfolded Walk	97

Catechumenate Connection Cross-Reference

Session	CCC Section	Topic	Tradition and/or Sacrament	Page
1st Lent (ABC)	1808	Temptation, Fortitude	Community, Eucharist	16
2nd Lent (ABC)	828, 2030	Risks of Faith, Saints	Saints, Baptism	21
3rd Lent (A)	694	Water	Water, Baptism	27
4th Lent (A)	1189, 1192	Light, Images	Light, Easter Vigil	39
5th Lent (A)	989	Resurrection	All Souls Day, Praying for the Dead	54
Palm Sunday (ABC)	N/A	Crucifixion, Suffering	Stations of the Cross	69
Easter Sunday (ABC)	640	Resurrection Gospel	Resurrection	77
2nd Easter (ABC)	830, 831	Catholic	Universality	81
	153	Gift of God	Gift of Faith	81
3rd Easter (AB)	1069	Liturgy	Liturgy	86, 90
3rd Easter (C)	873	Sharing Faith	Missions of the Church	96
4th Easter (ABC)	754	Church as Flock, Church Hierarchy, Listening to God	Holy Orders	100
5th Easter (A)	194, 195	Faith	Apostles' Creed, Nicene Creed	105
5th Easter (B)	2742, 2745	Prayer	Prayer	109
5th Easter (C)	2013	Love	Charity	114
6th Easter (ABC)	733–736	Holy Spirit	Holy Spirit	119
	232–234	Trinity	Sign of the Cross, Dove Symbolism	119
Ascension (ABC)	670	Discipleship	Vocations, Church History	124
7th Easter (ABC)	2746–2751	Prayer	Rosary	129
Pentecost (ABC)	696	Pentecost, Holy Spirit	Pentecostal Symbols, Holy Spirit	134

Cross-Reference by Section of the

Catechism of the Catholic Church

Section	Sacrament and/or Tradition	Topic	Sunday	Page
153	Gift of Faith	Gift of God	2nd Easter (ABC)	81
194, 195	Apostles' Creed, Nicene Creed	Faith	5th Easter (A)	105
232–234	Sign of the Cross, Dove Symbolism	Trinity	6th Easter (ABC)	119
640	Resurrection	Resurrection Gospel	Easter Sunday (ABC)	77
670	Vocations, Church History	Discipleship	Ascension (ABC)	124
694	Baptism, Water	Water	3rd Lent (A)	27
696	Pentecostal Symbols, Holy Spirit	Pentecost, Holy Spirit	Pentecost (ABC)	134
733–736	Holy Spirit	Holy Spirit	6th Easter (ABC)	119
754	Holy Orders	Church Hierarchy, Church as Flock, Listening to God	4th Easter (ABC)	100
828	Saints, Baptism	Risks of Faith, Saints	2nd Lent (ABC)	21
830, 831	Universality	Catholic	2nd Easter (ABC)	81
873	Missions of the Church	Sharing Faith	3rd Easter (C)	96
989	All Souls Day, Praying for the Dead	Resurrection	5th Lent (A)	54
1069	Liturgy	Liturgy	3rd Easter (AB)	86, 90
1808	Community, Eucharist	Temptation, Fortitude	1st Lent (ABC)	16
1189, 1192	Light, Easter Vigil	Light, Images	4th Lent (A)	39
2013	Charity	Love	5th Easter (C)	114
2030	Saints	Saints, Baptism	2nd Lent (ABC)	21
2742, 2745	Prayer	Prayer	5th Easter (B)	109
2746–2751	Rosary	Prayer	7th Easter (ABC)	129

Liturgical Calendar

For the Lent and Easter Seasons

Note: Some dioceses use the Ascension Sunday readings as a substitute for the Seventh Sunday of Easter readings.

2002 Year A		2003 Year B	
2/17	First Sunday of Lent	3/9	First Sunday of Lent
2/24	Second Sunday of Lent	3/16	Second Sunday of Lent
3/3	Third Sunday of Lent	3/23	Third Sunday of Lent
3/10	Fourth Sunday of Lent	3/30	Fourth Sunday of Lent
3/17	Fifth Sunday of Lent	4/6	Fifth Sunday of Lent
3/24	Palm Sunday	4/13	Palm Sunday
3/31	Easter	4/20	Easter
4/7	Second Sunday of Easter	4/27	Second Sunday of Easter
4/14	Third Sunday of Easter	5/4	Third Sunday of Easter
4/21	Fourth Sunday of Easter	5/11	Fourth Sunday of Easter
4/28	Fifth Sunday of Easter	5/18	Fifth Sunday of Easter
5/5	Sixth Sunday of Easter	5/25	Sixth Sunday of Easter
5/12	Seventh Sunday of Easter	6/1	Seventh Sunday of Easter
5/19	Pentecost	6/8	Pentecost

2004 Year C		2005 Year A	
2/29	First Sunday of Lent	2/13	First Sunday of Lent
3/7	Second Sunday of Lent	2/20	Second Sunday of Lent
3/14	Third Sunday of Lent	2/27	Third Sunday of Lent
3/21	Fourth Sunday of Lent	3/6	Fourth Sunday of Lent
3/28	Fifth Sunday of Lent	3/13	Fifth Sunday of Lent
4/4	Palm Sunday	3/20	Palm Sunday
4/11	Easter	3/27	Easter
4/18	Second Sunday of Easter	4/3	Second Sunday of Easter
4/25	Third Sunday of Easter	4/10	Third Sunday of Easter
5/2	Fourth Sunday of Easter	4/17	Fourth Sunday of Easter
5/9	Fifth Sunday of Easter	4/24	Fifth Sunday of Easter
5/16	Sixth Sunday of Easter	5/1	Sixth Sunday of Easter
5/23	Seventh Sunday of Easter	5/8	Seventh Sunday of Easter
5/30	Pentecost	5/15	Pentecost

2006 Year B		2007 Year C	
3/5	First Sunday of Lent	2/25	First Sunday of Lent
3/12	Second Sunday of Lent	3/4	Second Sunday of Lent
3/19	Third Sunday of Lent	3/11	Third Sunday of Lent
3/26	Fourth Sunday of Lent	3/18	Fourth Sunday of Lent
4/2	Fifth Sunday of Lent	3/25	Fifth Sunday of Lent
4/9	Palm Sunday	4/1	Palm Sunday
4/16	Easter	4/8	Easter
4/23	Second Sunday of Easter	4/15	Second Sunday of Easter
4/30	Third Sunday of Easter	4/22	Third Sunday of Easter
5/7	Fourth Sunday of Easter	4/29	Fourth Sunday of Easter
5/14	Fifth Sunday of Easter	5/6	Fifth Sunday of Easter
5/21	Sixth Sunday of Easter	5/13	Sixth Sunday of Easter
5/28	Seventh Sunday of Easter	5/20	Seventh Sunday of Easter
6/4	Pentecost	5/27	Pentecost

2008 Year A		2009 Year B	
2/10	First Sunday of Lent	3/1	First Sunday of Lent
2/17	Second Sunday of Lent	3/8	Second Sunday of Lent
2/24	Third Sunday of Lent	3/15	Third Sunday of Lent
3/2	Fourth Sunday of Lent	3/22	Fourth Sunday of Lent
3/9	Fifth Sunday of Lent	3/29	Fifth Sunday of Lent
3/16	Palm Sunday	4/5	Palm Sunday
3/23	Easter	4/12	Easter
3/30	Second Sunday of Easter	4/19	Second Sunday of Easter
4/6	Third Sunday of Easter	4/26	Third Sunday of Easter
4/13	Fourth Sunday of Easter	5/3	Fourth Sunday of Easter
4/20	Fifth Sunday of Easter	5/10	Fifth Sunday of Easter
4/27	Sixth Sunday of Easter	5/17	Sixth Sunday of Easter
5/4	Seventh Sunday of Easter	5/24	Seventh Sunday of Easter
5/11	Pentecost	5/31	Pentecost

2010 Year C		2011 Year A	
2/21	First Sunday of Lent	3/13	First Sunday of Lent
2/28	Second Sunday of Lent	3/20	Second Sunday of Lent
3/7	Third Sunday of Lent	3/27	Third Sunday of Lent
3/14	Fourth Sunday of Lent	4/3	Fourth Sunday of Lent
3/21	Fifth Sunday of Lent	4/10	Fifth Sunday of Lent
3/28	Palm Sunday	4/17	Palm Sunday
4/4	Easter	4/24	Easter
4/11	Second Sunday of Easter	5/1	Second Sunday of Easter
4/18	Third Sunday of Easter	5/8	Third Sunday of Easter
4/25	Fourth Sunday of Easter	5/15	Fourth Sunday of Easter
5/2	Fifth Sunday of Easter	5/22	Fifth Sunday of Easter
5/9	Sixth Sunday of Easter	5/29	Sixth Sunday of Easter
5/16	Seventh Sunday of Easter	6/5	Seventh Sunday of Easter
5/23	Pentecost	6/12	Pentecost

2012 Year B		2013 Year C	
2/26	First Sunday of Lent	2/17	First Sunday of Lent
3/4	Second Sunday of Lent	2/24	Second Sunday of Lent
3/11	Third Sunday of Lent	3/3	Third Sunday of Lent
3/18	Fourth Sunday of Lent	3/10	Fourth Sunday of Lent
3/25	Fifth Sunday of Lent	3/17	Fifth Sunday of Lent
4/1	Palm Sunday	3/24	Palm Sunday
4/8	Easter	3/31	Easter
4/15	Second Sunday of Easter	4/7	Second Sunday of Easter
4/22	Third Sunday of Easter	4/14	Third Sunday of Easter
4/29	Fourth Sunday of Easter	4/21	Fourth Sunday of Easter
5/6	Fifth Sunday of Easter	4/28	Fifth Sunday of Easter
5/13	Sixth Sunday of Easter	5/5	Sixth Sunday of Easter
5/20	Seventh Sunday of Easter	5/12	Seventh Sunday of Easter
5/27	Pentecost	5/19	Pentecost

2014 Year A		2015 Year B	
3/9	First Sunday of Lent	2/22	First Sunday of Lent
3/16	Second Sunday of Lent	3/1	Second Sunday of Lent
3/23	Third Sunday of Lent	3/8	Third Sunday of Lent
3/30	Fourth Sunday of Lent	3/15	Fourth Sunday of Lent
4/6	Fifth Sunday of Lent	3/22	Fifth Sunday of Lent
4/13	Palm Sunday	3/29	Palm Sunday
4/20	Easter	4/5	Easter
4/27	Second Sunday of Easter	4/12	Second Sunday of Easter
5/4	Third Sunday of Easter	4/19	Third Sunday of Easter
5/11	Fourth Sunday of Easter	4/26	Fourth Sunday of Easter
5/18	Fifth Sunday of Easter	5/3	Fifth Sunday of Easter
5/25	Sixth Sunday of Easter	5/10	Sixth Sunday of Easter
6/1	Seventh Sunday of Easter	5/17	Seventh Sunday of Easter
6/8	Pentecost	5/24	Pentecost

2016 Year C		2017 Year A	
2/14	First Sunday of Lent	3/5	First Sunday of Lent
2/21	Second Sunday of Lent	3/12	Second Sunday of Lent
2/28	Third Sunday of Lent	3/19	Third Sunday of Lent
3/6	Fourth Sunday of Lent	3/26	Fourth Sunday of Lent
3/13	Fifth Sunday of Lent	4/2	Fifth Sunday of Lent
3/20	Palm Sunday	4/9	Palm Sunday
3/27	Easter	4/16	Easter
4/3	Second Sunday of Easter	4/23	Second Sunday of Easter
4/10	Third Sunday of Easter	4/30	Third Sunday of Easter
4/17	Fourth Sunday of Easter	5/7	Fourth Sunday of Easter
4/24	Fifth Sunday of Easter	5/14	Fifth Sunday of Easter
5/1	Sixth Sunday of Easter	5/21	Sixth Sunday of Easter
5/8	Seventh Sunday of Easter	5/28	Seventh Sunday of Easter
5/15	Pentecost	6/4	Pentecost

2018 Year B		2019 Year C	
2/18	First Sunday of Lent	3/10	First Sunday of Lent
2/25	Second Sunday of Lent	3/17	Second Sunday of Lent
3/4	Third Sunday of Lent	3/24	Third Sunday of Lent
3/11	Fourth Sunday of Lent	3/31	Fourth Sunday of Lent
3/18	Fifth Sunday of Lent	4/7	Fifth Sunday of Lent
3/25	Palm Sunday	4/14	Palm Sunday
4/1	Easter	4/21	Easter
4/8	Second Sunday of Easter	4/28	Second Sunday of Easter
4/15	Third Sunday of Easter	5/5	Third Sunday of Easter
4/22	Fourth Sunday of Easter	5/12	Fourth Sunday of Easter
4/29	Fifth Sunday of Easter	5/19	Fifth Sunday of Easter
5/6	Sixth Sunday of Easter	5/26	Sixth Sunday of Easter
5/13	Seventh Sunday of Easter	6/2	Seventh Sunday of Easter
5/20	Pentecost	6/9	Pentecost

2020 Year A		2021 Year B	
3/1	First Sunday of Lent	2/21	First Sunday of Lent
3/8	Second Sunday of Lent	2/28	Second Sunday of Lent
3/15	Third Sunday of Lent	3/7	Third Sunday of Lent
3/22	Fourth Sunday of Lent	3/14	Fourth Sunday of Lent
3/29	Fifth Sunday of Lent	3/21	Fifth Sunday of Lent
4/5	Palm Sunday	3/28	Palm Sunday
4/12	Easter	4/4	Easter
4/19	Second Sunday of Easter	4/11	Second Sunday of Easter
4/26	Third Sunday of Easter	4/18	Third Sunday of Easter
5/3	Fourth Sunday of Easter	4/25	Fourth Sunday of Easter
5/10	Fifth Sunday of Easter	5/2	Fifth Sunday of Easter
5/17	Sixth Sunday of Easter	5/9	Sixth Sunday of Easter
5/24	Seventh Sunday of Easter	5/16	Seventh Sunday of Easter
5/31	Pentecost	5/23	Pentecost

2022 Year C		2023 Year A	
3/6	First Sunday of Lent	2/26	First Sunday of Lent
3/13	Second Sunday of Lent	3/5	Second Sunday of Lent
3/20	Third Sunday of Lent	3/12	Third Sunday of Lent
3/27	Fourth Sunday of Lent	3/19	Fourth Sunday of Lent
4/3	Fifth Sunday of Lent	3/26	Fifth Sunday of Lent
4/10	Palm Sunday	4/2	Palm Sunday
4/17	Easter	4/9	Easter
4/24	Second Sunday of Easter	4/16	Second Sunday of Easter
5/1	Third Sunday of Easter	4/23	Third Sunday of Easter
5/8	Fourth Sunday of Easter	4/30	Fourth Sunday of Easter
5/15	Fifth Sunday of Easter	5/7	Fifth Sunday of Easter
5/22	Sixth Sunday of Easter	5/14	Sixth Sunday of Easter
5/29	Seventh Sunday of Easter	5/21	Seventh Sunday of Easter
6/5	Pentecost	5/28	Pentecost

2024 Year B		2025 Year C	
2/18	First Sunday of Lent	3/9	First Sunday of Lent
2/25	Second Sunday of Lent	3/16	Second Sunday of Lent
3/3	Third Sunday of Lent	3/23	Third Sunday of Lent
3/10	Fourth Sunday of Lent	3/30	Fourth Sunday of Lent
3/17	Fifth Sunday of Lent	4/6	Fifth Sunday of Lent
3/24	Palm Sunday	4/13	Palm Sunday
3/31	Easter	4/20	Easter
4/7	Second Sunday of Easter	4/27	Second Sunday of Easter
4/14	Third Sunday of Easter	5/4	Third Sunday of Easter
4/21	Fourth Sunday of Easter	5/11	Fourth Sunday of Easter
4/28	Fifth Sunday of Easter	5/18	Fifth Sunday of Easter
5/5	Sixth Sunday of Easter	5/25	Sixth Sunday of Easter
5/12	Seventh Sunday of Easter	6/1	Seventh Sunday of Easter
5/19	Pentecost	6/8	Pentecost

2026 Year A		2027 Year B	
2/22	First Sunday of Lent	2/14	First Sunday of Lent
3/1	Second Sunday of Lent	2/21	Second Sunday of Lent
3/8	Third Sunday of Lent	2/28	Third Sunday of Lent
3/15	Fourth Sunday of Lent	3/7	Fourth Sunday of Lent
3/22	Fifth Sunday of Lent	3/14	Fifth Sunday of Lent
3/29	Palm Sunday	3/21	Palm Sunday
4/5	Easter	3/28	Easter
4/12	Second Sunday of Easter	4/4	Second Sunday of Easter
4/19	Third Sunday of Easter	4/11	Third Sunday of Easter
4/26	Fourth Sunday of Easter	4/18	Fourth Sunday of Easter
5/3	Fifth Sunday of Easter	4/25	Fifth Sunday of Easter
5/10	Sixth Sunday of Easter	5/2	Sixth Sunday of Easter
5/17	Seventh Sunday of Easter	5/9	Seventh Sunday of Easter
5/24	Pentecost	5/16	Pentecost

2028 Year C		2029 Year A	
3/5	First Sunday of Lent	2/18	First Sunday of Lent
3/12	Second Sunday of Lent	2/25	Second Sunday of Lent
3/19	Third Sunday of Lent	3/4	Third Sunday of Lent
3/26	Fourth Sunday of Lent	3/11	Fourth Sunday of Lent
4/2	Fifth Sunday of Lent	3/18	Fifth Sunday of Lent
4/9	Palm Sunday	3/25	Palm Sunday
4/16	Easter	4/1	Easter
4/23	Second Sunday of Easter	4/8	Second Sunday of Easter
4/30	Third Sunday of Easter	4/15	Third Sunday of Easter
5/7	Fourth Sunday of Easter	4/22	Fourth Sunday of Easter
5/14	Fifth Sunday of Easter	4/29	Fifth Sunday of Easter
5/21	Sixth Sunday of Easter	5/6	Sixth Sunday of Easter
5/28	Seventh Sunday of Easter	5/13	Seventh Sunday of Easter
6/4	Pentecost	5/20	Pentecost

2030 Year B	
3/10	First Sunday of Lent
3/17	Second Sunday of Lent
3/24	Third Sunday of Lent
3/31	Fourth Sunday of Lent
4/7	Fifth Sunday of Lent
4/14	Palm Sunday
4/21	Easter
4/28	Second Sunday of Easter
5/5	Third Sunday of Easter
5/12	Fourth Sunday of Easter
5/19	Fifth Sunday of Easter
5/26	Sixth Sunday of Easter
6/2	Seventh Sunday of Easter
6/9	Pentecost